RUMINATA

"The Sexual Theory of Everything"
and Other Apostasies

W. Grey Champion

Ruminata: "The Sexual Theory of Everything" and Other Apostasies
Copyright © 2022 by W. Grey Champion

All rights reserved. This book or any portion thereof may not be reproduced or used in any manner whatsoever without the express written permission of the publisher, except for the use of brief quotations in a book review.

Printed in the United States of America

Luminare Press
442 Charnelton St.
Eugene, OR 97401
www.luminarepress.com

LCCN: 2022911177
ISBN: 978-1-64388-949-8

TABLE OF CONTENTS

Preface 1
Introduction 9

The Sexual Theory of Everything 13
On Buddhism 28
Decline and Fall 42
Breeding 53
Marriage and Children 62
Choices 72
Modernism 84
The Piano Teacher 96
The Reign of Sport 108
Appearance and Reality 117
Potlatch 127
Misogyny 133
Communication 144
Travel 154
Just Call Me Alice 163
Aging 174
Death and Euthanasia 185
The Phases of Life 194

Epilogue 203
Bibliography 208
Author Bio 211

Preface

Early in the month of May in 1945, the great cataclysm of World War II ended in Europe with the surrender of Germany. By the end of summer, conflict had ceased as well on the Pacific front. After six terrible years of war, survivors were jubilant, free at last to carry on with their lives, plans, and dreams. Soldiers came home to their sweethearts, returned to civilian jobs, bought houses, and settled down to raise their children, many of whom were born the very next year.

I was not among that baby boom, having been born in February 1945, a bit too soon. I mention this fact by way of introducing these essays only because in retrospect I realize that the outlook and attitudes reflected here have been shaped or at least influenced by that tsunami of contemporaries, which impacted my experiences in life. Hordes of somewhat younger people were always behind me, sometimes walking in my footsteps, sometimes pushing me in untoward ways. I no sooner would discover a quiet inn in Maine than it would begin filling up months in advance, tribes of cyclists descending on it, then cruise ship passengers clogging the streets of town. A creature of habit, set in my ways, I would go to replace old, worn draperies only to find that the pinch pleated drape on a traverse rod could not be found, as the young people had turned to Roman shades and then to "window treatments." Even worse aggravation surrounded changing fashions in bedding.

The legacy of that postwar generation is mixed. They succeeded in many positive innovations and social reforms, yet the weight of their numbers worked against them. Their vast cohort grew up and reproduced; their children grew and reproduced and then their children's children. Schools were overcrowded, enormous sports stadia filled and likewise rock concerts, cities bulged with people living cheek by jowl. Water and air became polluted, and at some point, the climate was seen to be changing, causing aberrant, destructive weather patterns and serious, irreversible damage to planet Earth.

Despite the argument that in the modern era, value lies in technological savvy and not musty atavisms, the fabric of human society has from prehistoric times depended upon the accumulation and preservation of the knowledge, experience, and wisdom handed down as lore. This fact will always be true, as true as the aphorism that those who do not know history are doomed to repeat it. My hope in the essays collected here is to address the newer generations especially, to tell of lessons learned and pitfalls of which to beware. Cleverly inventive, the young people today may know the many intricacies of the smartphone, transition smoothly into whatever software update Silicon Valley throws at them, and be up on all the internet memes, but should they trust the wisdom of an algorithm in choosing a mate? Do they understand the realities of married life, parenthood, and growing old? With no basis for comparison, can they imagine how much simpler life used to be before the high tech they value so highly prevailed—in other words, before they were born? Should this collection of personal essays succeed in reaching young readers, or even the not-so young, my purpose is to aid them in averting the consequences of their potential errancy. The wiser among them will understand the impossibility of knowing the true, firsthand reality of history and the risks of not knowing. For them I offer these reflections in all humility yet not without some urgency.

My life began in that postwar period of growing prosperity and rising hopes. Peace brought industry and enterprise, invention and creativity, and higher standards and expectations. Then came the sixties, with protest movements upending centuries of social traditions. Along with bigotry and hypocrisy, young people threw discipline and conformity to the winds. Women would be liberated, schools integrated, and poor people educated, while on the way, rules would be defied and standards scorned. As I near the twilight of this life, I am forced to acknowledge that for all the social good brought about in those years, there has been unforeseen decline. The generation that overturned the old rules and repudiated their elders does not have the legitimacy to command respect from their own children. It is a dangerous heritage, addressed in these essays.

Now as I write, the "boomers" are growing old. Not surprisingly, the personal memoir is a growing genre, especially since the internet has so facilitated the ability to publish a book, write a blog, post a video, and leave one's words and thoughts afloat in cyberspace for intergalactic travelers to discover. In this collection, the essay on communication describes the dubious value of the tidal wave of books that has resulted, yet for those like myself who enjoy writing and have lived to an age when the horizon of this earthly existence draws closer, the urge is strong to take a shot in the dark, tossing one's message onto the choppy seas in a corked bottle. If it aids one other person, living or yet to be born, why not?

These essays, however, are not intended as a memoir. The subject matter covers a variety of topics that have interested me all my life and reflects my inclination to challenge prevailing wisdom, to test ingrained assumptions. The essays are arguments, hence the subtitle, but more fundamentally ruminations, hence the title. From the Latin meaning "to chew the cud," to *ruminate* is to mull over something slowly and thoughtfully. For readers of a contemplative nature, I offer much on which to chew. I hope further that those holding strong contrary opinions will find something more to consider.

Historically, the essay as a literary form has been something of a catchall. I use it in one sense of several dictionary definitions: "An analytic or interpretive literary composition usually dealing with its subject from a limited or personal point of view." As a verb, it means "to try, to attempt…an initial tentative effort." Thus these essays present my personal point of view, and with them, I *essay* to support my views, especially those that may strike readers as outré.

In offering them, I am sensitive to the impression of arrogance an author may give, even unwittingly, in the absence of opposing arguments. I have tried not to use a bullhorn but rather to emphasize, where needed, my ownership of opinions and the basis for them.

In the course of putting my thoughts together, I came across a most informative book on the subject of essays themselves. *Essayism: On Form, Feeling, and Nonfiction* was written in 2017 by Irish academician Brian Dillon. His book gives numerous examples from Montaigne in the sixteenth century to Joan Didion and the author's personal favorite, Susan Sontag. In general, he appears to see the essay as a rambling, digressive form that is more about style than subject matter, reflecting his focus on the informal essay, particularly the type of short memoir of a fiction writer. He gives only a nod to the formal essay, explaining that he is "allergic to polemics."

It will be obvious from the following ruminations that I have no such allergy, and I try not to ramble or digress. A most helpful quote that Dillon includes in his book is from *Minima Moralia*, a 1951 work by German philosopher Theodor Adorno: "Anyone wishing to express something is so carried away by it that he ceases to reflect on it. Too close to his intention in his thoughts, he forgets to say what he wants to say" (Dillon 2017, 83). That is the pitfall I have been stepping gingerly around in writing these essays—with some degree of success, I hope. I try to keep to the point and to assure it is communicated, in the final analysis, to the reader.

Even so, futility is a natural concern, given the aforementioned cacophony of the digital age. Years ago when my aging father was hospitalized and my mother was staying with me, I gave her a tape recorder—the old-fashioned kind with actual tape—and urged her to pass the time recording her life history for the benefit of descendants. Having the Irish gift of storytelling, she took on the project with relish, and I still cherish the result. My father, however, the pragmatic German, could see no point, arguing when he came out of hospital that young people would have no interest in the past, even of their own family. Recalling his skepticism, I am bemused these days whenever I see a commercial for a genealogy website. No interest indeed! When people are young, they are too busy surviving to take an interest in anything. In short order, they start to show some gray in the beard and around the fringes, and nostalgia builds along with curiosity.

I am not interested, however, in telling my life story, which, should anyone seek to know it after I am gone, will be there in my journals and diaries. My concern in gathering these ruminations is to address questions I have faced that might have been answered by an older generation had it not assiduously demurred, presuming my disinterest. I might have been prepared if only someone had told me, for example, about certain aspects of the aging process. I might have reconsidered decisions made in youthful innocence, given an older person's wise advice, instead of having to live with consequences I could not foresee. When I was too young to know what to ask, why did they not tell me, before passing into that inaccessible realm of death, what I needed to know?

I believe common stereotypes render people reluctant. Young people are regarded as apathetic and self-centered, and old people are foolish, particularly in their penchant for giving unsolicited advice. Easy as it may be to think in terms of such generalities—I confess guilt myself—we all know they are not universally applicable. I intend to speak up, foolish or not. May it not be said of me that I hesitated, leaving things unsaid. At least future generations will have a reference book if they are patient enough to find it in the digital haystack that is Google or Amazon.

The substance of the essays reflects my conviction that the purpose of life, taking particular advantage of human potential, is to learn. I never sought to acquire a large fund of knowledge, however, nor did I aspire to the concomitant credentials. Instead, my aim has always been to discover the meaning of things at the deepest possible level. Often I have looked to science, which has probed the depths since ancient times and has been increasingly instructive in the modern era. I neglected neither philosophy nor religion, giving particular attention to works that overlapped with the sciences. My early reading, as I outline in the essay "On Buddhism," included Aldous Huxley, Bertrand de Jouvenel, Konrad Lorenz, and Pierre Teilhard de Chardin, the latter's 1955 book *The Phenomenon of Man* being especially influential on the subject of civilization.

The deeper question of life itself, where and how it began, remained. Life and death are equally mysterious to us. Depending on our inclination, we tend to leave the matter to science or religion, and an article in a science periodical gave me a clue. Exploring the origins of life in the early days of Earth, researchers pointed to the organic compounds made possible by the abundance of carbon. The point in those vast stretches of time when these compounds evolved the capacity to self-replicate is when science recognizes the first sign of life. That became the subject of the first essay, "The Sexual Theory of Everything."

When in 1979 I was introduced to Buddhism by the Zen classic, *Zen Mind, Beginner's Mind*, which conveys the teaching of Japanese master Shunryu Suzuki, founder of the San Francisco Zen Center, I saw no further reason to pursue Western philosophy or the established Western religions, which seemed primitive by comparison. Furthermore, advances in science were converging on Eastern thought, as I saw in such books as *The Tao of Physics* by Fritjof Capra. The essay "On Buddhism" deals with the astonishing relevance of that ancient faith, a recurring theme in other essays as well.

The subjects I have chosen to ruminate upon will be familiar to anyone who has followed my blog, *From the Moleskine*, to which I have posted each week for many years. Here several of the topics are discussed at greater length. The thresholds of this life are of particular concern, the struggles and decisions they pose. Often I am questioning of accepted truisms and skeptical of entrenched attitudes on what is correct and proper. I do not intend to be iconoclastic but seek only to challenge certain shibboleths of modern society and culture lest the young generation fall prey to avoidable mistakes. For example, in the interest of multicultural diversity, may we not in many cases do a disservice to the young by not impressing upon them the difficulties of intermarriage between races or religions? In our eagerness to avoid reinforcing stereotypes with respect to ethnicity, do we deny a certain validity to their origins?

The essays "Breeding" and "Marriage and Children" tweak the immoderate excesses of political correctness. I am well aware that in the social climate in which I am writing, critics will claim to discern here only carefully nuanced prejudices or, more harshly, thinly veiled bigotry. Anticipating them, my retort is that while idealism is a beautiful thing, its mortal enemy throughout history has been reality. Temper idealism with realism, specifically about human nature, and maybe humankind has a fighting chance of preserving civilization, which invariably collapses upon the resurgent barbarity of tribalism. Like wolves that run with the pack, we are a social species and would do well, individually and collectively, to understand, acknowledge, and deal with the ramifications. Our prehistoric tribal nature is a recurring theme in several of these essays and the main theme in "Decline and Fall."

In keeping with the sometimes rambling nature of rumination, suggesting "little of either purposive thought or rapt absorption," as it says in Webster's, my attention does wander off into discourses on the arts, fashion, and sports. In "Modernism," "The Reign of Sport," "Appearance, and Reality," for example, my object is to contrast past and present, inspiring in some readers more considered attitudes about their future direction. I include an interview with an old friend who taught piano for some decades before retiring a few years back. "The Piano Teacher" is a delicious exposé for which she begs to remain anonymous, but I will venture to say that everything I know about music theory, I learned from her. We share a passion for the Pythagorean scale!

I may come off as a crusty old curmudgeon touting his antiquated ideas from a soapbox on the town green, but a certain freedom from propriety goes along with advancing age. When one has had a long life, led by curiosity to delve into topics of particular interest, he may write of these things from a personal point of view. The essay is such a form that should not be approached as a scholarly treatise. I have attempted to be as factual as possible, but my aim is not exhaustive discussion. On any one of these topics, there are doubtless heavy tomes compiled by erudite academicians for whom a single subject has been their singular discipline, and I beg not to diminish their admirable contributions. I have come across many, in working on this collection, that I list in the bibliography, and where I have quoted these, you will find the page numbers in parentheses. Other sources are footnoted. In contrast, these thoughts and opinions are simply based on my reading and personal experiences, offered humbly to posterity.

The essays may overlap to some extent, though I have tried not to be repetitive. You will nevertheless discern recurring themes including the overpopulation of our species, under-appreciated aspects of human nature, ways in which Buddhism relates to our lives, and a general tendency to take issue not only with modernity but also its ill-considered cultural axioms.

As my hope has been to amuse as well as edify, feel free to skip about as your mood inclines. Take a gladsome tour of the looking glass world in the essay "Just Call Me Alice," contemplate five hundred varieties of yogurt in "Choices," and consider my modest proposal in "Misogyny" for eliminating the female gender—á la Jonathan Swift. Curl up on the sofa or recline in your easy chair to ruminate—and enjoy!

W. Grey Champion
May 2020

Introduction

IN THE EARLY MONTHS OF 2020, AS THIS COMPILATION OF ESSAYS was nearing completion, rumors were trickling in about a new virus jumping species from bats to humans in Wuhan, the largest city in central China. A coronavirus related to severe acute respiratory syndrome (SARS) was causing a terrible respiratory disease dubbed COVID-19. Given the lightning speed of information and the global nature of air travel, people fled the disease, spreading it worldwide. There existed no human immunity for this novel virus, and it soon became evident that it was highly infectious and much more potentially lethal than seasonal flu. The only protections against it were the measures used since ancient times against the plagues to which we have been historically vulnerable: isolation of the sick and avoidance of all human contact. In modern terms, lockdown.

By March, international air travel had virtually ceased. All the giant cruise ships idled in whatever safe harbor was available, whole countries in Europe were shut down, closed for business, and trade and supply chains groaned under the strain. Plants and factories, stores, schools, and offices struggled to adjust as fear spread along with the pathogen. In the worst outbreaks, hospitals filled beyond capacity and morgues likewise. The economy, now globally integrated, was thrown into a tailspin. A shroud of uncertainty descended over every human activity from simple daily interactions to the political and social fate of nations.

As a species, human beings are clever, enough certainly to be able to predict catastrophes and their probability. Even the best minds, however, cannot foresee *when* a cataclysm as universal as a pandemic will befall. Few in my generation thought they would be alive to see it, but here we are. Hoping for the best, we never seem to be prepared for the worst.

As the situation unfolded, I feared that several of the following essays, those that described the world before the pandemic, had become abruptly obsolete. It seemed that as long as the world was held in abeyance by this threat, there would be no certainty that the future would in any way resemble the past. Would the prodigiousness of world travel ever reach its former level? Could mortality from the virus and related causes reduce the population enough to nullify or suspend the several conditions it had been causing, which had recently seemed intractable? The pandemic itself was fostered by human crowding, the encroachment of habitation in wild spaces that brought animals in dangerous proximity to us. Surely we might have seen this coming and that quite speedily. I realized it was incumbent on me to revisit each essay with these dire considerations in mind.

The population globally had grown to more than seven billion, including more than a billion in India and China and hundreds of millions in the next most populous nations such as the United States and Brazil. For perspective, the influenza pandemic of 1918 had a death toll estimated as high as fifty million, representing 3–5 percent of the world population at the time. This coronavirus pandemic was unlikely to be as deadly, but even this could not be certain. Along with the sickness itself, the grip of uncertainty and fear of infection strangled the economy, adding to the morass.

As I went over the manuscript, I determined three things. First, any insight into human nature would stand as firmly as that unyielding nature itself. Second, because of that obdurate nature in us, pre-pandemic conditions could be counted on to resume as soon as feasible, and third, the common sense I have taken pains to convey in these essays will continue perennial as it always has. I was not in a rush to publish, yet sitting out in my yard, under the flight path of a major airport, I could not but note the gradual return of passenger jets flying over and was assured that all the excesses I here decry were bound to return with their inescapable results.

Sure enough, reopening was phased in by jurisdiction with certain critical adjustments to stop community spread of the virus. Masks would be worn, people would stand six feet apart, and large gatherings were forbidden. Restaurants could open for outdoor dining and schools for remote, virtual learning. Sporting events, which could not long be withheld from rabid fans, were being televised—no spectators. Team sports organizations tried to avoid contagion by isolating all members in a "bubble" with regular testing for the virus. Traffic on the freeways, gloriously light for those several months of lockdown, gradually picked up to its former outrageous levels.

No one sees the future. Clairvoyance, *clear seeing*, may be only the careful observation of causes, predicting the likely effects. If I have been clairvoyant, what I see is not so much a light at the end of this tunnel but a resumption of the accumulating disasters we faced before the pandemic. My sincere hope is that this book will survive to stimulate clear thinking on its various themes.

THE SEXUAL THEORY OF EVERYTHING

- Defining Life Itself -

The world is not ruled by men; it is ruled by sperm. Men believe themselves to be rational, in control of human affairs through the force of reason, but this belief is not borne out by experience or history. From the teleological perspective and contrary to appearances, the agenda of their germ cells, the sperm, guides their motivations, decisions, and actions, as any proper analysis would make clear.

Let me begin by saying that I come to this theory with a keen sense of disappointment, having been born and raised before the pill and the sexual revolution that signaled the inexorable decline of a more romantic time when sexual activity had a potential consequence far more dreadful than disease or death, i.e., inadvertent procreation. Having gained full control over this process, we have seen fit to dispense with all the beautiful traditions of courtship, the intense emotions, even the sacred commitment of marriage that once accompanied it. To those of us old enough to remember, this loss weighs with a heavy sadness; ironically, it has unmasked a harsh, ugly reality about humankind. Have we freed ourselves to lead a beautiful, rational life? No, just to have more sex. Modern birth control came with the hope that human beings would finally be able to keep the population within the limit of resources—food, water, space. Women who preferred a career over motherhood would have that option. Those who wanted fewer children would get their wish, and there would be balance—zero population growth. The fear of every puritanical soul, however, that now people would enjoy sex for pleasure alone, not reproduction as God intended, was unfounded. It was all about procreation after all. Women, career or not, kept giving birth, with one camp going so far as to denounce the ability to choose. In cultures that give women more rights, families do tend to be smaller, which directly reflects the agenda of that other germ cell, the ovum, further bolstering my theory about the source of all human motivation, but the intentionally childless remained rare.

In imitation of nuclear physics, wherein we see a perennial search for the Grand Unified Theory reconciling quantum mechanics to general relativity, let me set forth a unifying biosocial theory of everything. More accurately, it should be termed "reproductive," since sexual reproduction is a relative latecomer in evolution, but the sexual theory of everything is more tantalizing for reasons embedded in the theory.

DEFINING LIFE: THE SROCS

The first thing we must recognize, as every postmenopausal woman discovers, is that the phases of life are defined by reproduction. We grow into puberty, enter the mating and nesting phases, and then raise children until they also are able to reproduce. Finally losing that capability, we become irrelevant—at least to nature and often to family, friends, and society at large. Ask any retired person catching the look of surprise on acquaintances who apparently assumed he or she was dead. These life phases hold true even for those who fail to reproduce or cannot; witness homosexual couples mating, nesting, and growing old with an "empty nest" that was never otherwise.

The deep questions addressed by our religions and philosophies reflect the sense of impenetrable mystery with which life and its phases leaves us. When does it begin: at conception or birth? Is there an individual soul? Is there experience after death? Above all, what *is* death, described by Hamlet as that "undiscovered country from whose bourne no traveler returns"? What value or meaning can inhere in mortal beings who struggle through their brief lives only to slip into oblivion? Shakespeare offers much commentary on the human condition, none better than Macbeth's soliloquy: "Out, out brief candle! Life is but a walking shadow, a poor player who struts and frets his hour upon the stage and then is heard no more, a tale told by an idiot, signifying nothing."

    The inability to muster the means to adequately respond to those questions is painfully frustrating to the average person who has for the most part, in modern times, gradually turned away from the supernatural religions and drifted into a secular agnosticism or fatalistic despair. Convinced that such deep problems are beyond our abilities to solve, most people give up and, worse, close their ears and roll their eyes when the subject arises. We must not despair of the answers but try harder to find them, to look deeper and get to the core of things. The greatest question is not about death; we can readily see and define what it means to die, for organ systems to fail until consciousness is no longer sustained and vital processes cease. The key question is *what is life?* Science tells us to go back in an unbroken chain to the "primordial soup," that original sea of chemicals that produced the first organic compounds. Our planet was fortunate to have the right chemical ingredients, especially carbon atoms that were helpful in their proclivity to combine in forming those compounds. Atoms collected into molecules, molecules into cells with nuclei, and cells into organisms. Eons passed in the progress from one stage to the next, but at some point, beginning with RNA and later DNA, organic compounds evolved the ability to replicate.

    Let me emphasize there was no line crossed in the expression of this ability. There is no definitive point in this evolution where we can say, "Aha! Life!" In our enormously long hindsight, we can see that the stage where we begin to recognize self-replication is the stage to which we also start ascribing the quality "living." Self-replication stands as our definition of life from its origins. There still is debate around the fringes: Are viruses alive even though they must invade cells to perpetuate themselves? What about crystals that grow and replicate? Despite these gray areas, the mainstream of evolution flows from this ability to reproduce, because with it, the self-replicating organic compounds (let's call them SROCs) overflow the earth, continually adapting to better harness resources and thus perpetuate ad infinitum.

We humans are the most recent and finest (so far) temporal heirs of the original SROCs. No wonder the wise old wag is able to pronounce without exaggeration, "It really is all about sex, isn't it?" As I see it, the business of perpetuating and spreading one's kind has two aspects. First, it depends on replicating with some precision—in other words, duplicating oneself as closely as possible. The world of RNA fell short, allowing for too many unsuccessful mutations, and then the evolutionary process gave rise to DNA with its wondrously advanced replicative power. Second, species perpetuation benefits from some mutation, whereby life forms may adapt to the challenges of a fluctuating environment as they move into all the highly variable niches of this earth. At this point, the theory of evolution, obvious to most, becomes questionable to those who claim "intelligent design." How could the random mutations occurring so infrequently in DNA account for the precise matching of species to their peculiar niches? How is it that certain orchids are pollinated by only one kind of insect or that the coloration of birds is often specific to their particular habitats? The conclusion of skeptics—that eons of evolution could not have produced enough changes to bring these amazing results—leads them to the clear evidence of the hand of God. Evolutionary theory did not stand still after Darwin; it continued to evolve, and what now seems clear is that mutations are not random but that they respond in some way to the environment, likely involving the newly discovered chemical switches that determine which genes are turned on and when. There is always more to learn.

The evolving complexity of organisms brought the development of sexual reproduction, which allowed for still greater variety, enhancing in turn the ability to adapt and survive. As sexual beings, we combine our unique genetic material with that of one of the opposite gender to produce a child who is similar to both while identical to neither—the hand of God or a wonderful bit of karma. From this vantage point atop the tree of life, we can look back and still see the roots of it all, and as we observed, there are two: replicate as closely as possible to identity and leave room for change to survive the unforeseen. These are the rules—paradoxical and at times conflicting.

CIVILIZED SOCIETY

How does this basic information get to be a theory of everything? In *The Phenomenon of Man,* de Chardin uses the term *coalescence* to describe an odd similarity in observed processes with small units organizing into greater ones of progressive complexity. Atoms coalesce into molecules, molecules to cells, cells to organisms, organisms to societies, societies to civilizations, and hence, he extrapolated, to a future of world unity—his Omega Point in which, as a Jesuit, he envisioned the return of Christ. Let us pick up the thread where organisms have coalesced into societies, evolution having produced social species including *Homo sapiens*. Early man and his predecessors lived for millions of years in small kinship groups, a tribal state that more or less accommodated the aforementioned rules. First, the tribe defined a reproductive circle with shared DNA, allowing the individual to select a mate with whom he would be able nearly to clone himself. Second, interplay among tribes reduced inbreeding. Even warfare over limited resources enlivened the gene pool through capture and enslavement. Since the species survived and flourished, it appears that war was less destructive than inbreeding would have been. Then came civilization, with its wholesale conquests, in climates that allowed for more stable means of survival.

Civilization is the latest and highest expression of coalescence that social species have attained. Tribes have been brought together through some degree of coercion—living, trading, and interbreeding at the behest of the overlords, the pharaohs, the Romans, the British, or the Soviets. Nations may be a smaller manifestation of this phenomenon of civilization, being larger than tribes while retaining some tribal qualities. Notice with the breakup of the Soviet empire how every ancient tribal group sought to be an "independent *nation*." A tribe is a tribe, and civilizations run aground eventually through the resurgence of tribalism. The nation state might be considered the first evidence of regression.

Bear in mind that in the perspective of prehistory, civilization, even from what we consider its ancient beginnings, is the tip of the iceberg. With the start of civilization, mankind loses sight of—indeed rejects—its primitive origins, taking on a lofty and distorted opinion of itself. Undeniably, humans have great potential, whether positive or negative, but human nature remains rooted—and must always—in the nature of life itself as it must be defined. Tribal life satisfied that nature successfully for millions of years, while civilization goes against the grain, attempting to dissolve tribal barriers, to stir the pot. In so doing, there ceases to be a comfortably defined reproductive circle from which to choose a mate and no way to distinguish "us" from "them." Observe how people in modern society try to group themselves into smaller units—a church, a club, or a gang. No better example of the SROCs at work are the cafeteria lunch tables of an "integrated" school: here are the black students together, there the white, and there the Asian. We may sit together in the classrooms, but when it comes to a social life, to the serious business of mating, something within us seeks to replicate as closely as possible to identity.

This is by no means a defense of racism. To the contrary, blessings on those courageous few who intermarry, thanks to whom we may all eventually look alike. Then and only then, when there is nothing to discriminate, may discrimination come to an end. As a civilization expands and matures, it is increasingly marked by the dilution of the fundamental, primal needs of the tribe and thereby threatened with internal collapse as these needs reassert themselves. The first civilization to survive the resurgence of tribalism will be the one that recognizes and finds the means to accommodate the agenda of the SROCs: to incorporate the cohesion within tribes while avoiding the violence between them. That would require rational thought, and as I set forth in the first paragraph, the real drivers of human behavior are not found in the brain. Einstein famously wondered whether while being free to do what we will, we are free to *will* what we will. He was on to something. The brain allows us free will, but ever so subtly, unconscious and unacknowledged, the sperm and the ova are telling the brain what to will.

SEXUAL POLITICS

Thus, boys and girls, a remedial review of the birds and the bees. The female of the species carries a finite number of ova, dispensed one per month during the limited years of fertility. She is driven to find a mate capable of supporting and protecting her children but only as many as she feels capable of carefully nurturing. By contrast, the male produces countless sperm that swim fast and, as it turns out, compete among themselves. Their agenda is to procreate as widely as possible. The conflict inherent in the opposite genders, which must come together to perpetuate the species, is mediated through the institution of marriage—society's invention to protect women and children—which is not only a union between two people but a union of opposites, people who differ in the fundamental physiological and psychological ways I have described. Because society has such a stake in future generations, marriage is peculiar to heterosexuals. Gay marriage, while now legal in more enlightened societies, is by definition a union of two people who are fundamentally the same. Nonetheless, such couples and their children may expect to incur all the associated legal complexities society imposes through marriage.

Most instructive on this same subject is the abortion controversy, overheated in the extreme, and why? Why are males most especially livid at the thought of women controlling their reproductive lives? For the female, led by her limited and thus precious germ cells, the right to terminate an unwanted pregnancy is useful; if a fourth child would strain the capacity to raise the first three, better to abort. The male, whose agenda is written by those rabid, eager little sperm, is enormously threatened if the pregnancy he initiated can be ended. How will his DNA become widespread in the population? Sperm are not concerned with raising children, only producing as many as possible. I venture to say that were this not so, the world would not be overpopulated with our species to the point of overwhelming the resources needed for its survival. I am speaking in generalities, which while readily refuted anecdotally, may nonetheless retain validity. Moreover, I am not asserting that people consciously consider such strategies, merely addressing the root causes of their actions and behavior.

We must realize that when the ability to replicate evolved, there was nothing to limit reproductive potential except competition for resources. As a result, the myriad species that came into being over the eons, in the innumerable niches the planet offered, adapted to one another, forming what we now refer to as the balance of nature, which is fundamentally the food chain. Plant life captures the energy of the sun, converting it through photosynthesis. Ungulates live off the plants, in the process keeping vegetation in check. Atop the pyramid, carnivorous predators kill to eat, ensuring that the herds of herbivores do not overpopulate. None of this behavior is intentional but brought about through causes and conditions. What nature exhibits is agency without intention, intelligence without a brain, as when trees communicate through their roots in response to environmental stresses.

In nature, only the apex predators, few in number, live to die of old age. That includes *Homo sapiens*, but we have cleverly subverted the balance of nature as it applies to us. We are able to control our numbers; we do not, as I argue, because the bases of our reproductive behavior are intrinsic to life. Instead, we debate the question of whether life begins at conception or birth when in reality, life is a chain unbroken from the beginning. We have seen it was not something instilled but a *quality* that emerged, one that we define in retrospect, distinguishing it from nonlife. It is startling to think of life as a form of nonlife, as I will discuss later, but the living and the nonliving are made of the same stuff, the same atoms and molecules. Primitive humans retained a sense of this unity, ascribing spirit to the rocks, the waters, the clouds. We only call it "life" when it evolves the ability to replicate itself.

For all its flaws, sexual reproduction allows for the wonder of genetic variety we witness in humankind, while the first rule of the SROCs—to replicate as close to identity as possible—is met by choosing a partner from one's small circle, one's tribe. Once we recognize the tribe as a direct consequence of a life force defined by self-replication—precise self-replication—the imprint of my theory becomes clear in matters large and small, from those cafeteria lunch tables to international conflicts. Are there any of these latter that *cannot* be traced to tribalism? Is there any maniacal dictator who cannot be compared to a strutting rooster or an alpha baboon, proclaiming supreme reproductive rights based on superior strength? Is there any marital friction that does not boil down, in some way, to "my clan is better than yours"?

RELIGION AND POLITICAL PHILOSOPHY

How can a Sexual Theory of Everything encompass religion? I believe an alien from outer space, upon learning of the religious pillars of Western civilization, would be forgiven for concluding that Judaism is all about food—what to eat when and under what circumstances—and Christianity is about sex—who to have it with, how often, and upon what authority. Religion, at least at the level of the practitioner, is very much about social sanctions that provide for tribal cohesion and thus for the legacy of the SROCs. The threat to this primal legacy from modern civilization, with its birth control, its feminism, its isolation in anonymity, and the degrading power of its irresistible telecommunications, has given rise to fundamentalism in all the world's religions. Unsurprisingly, Islam has taken the most violent offense, leading to terrorism, the worm at the core of our apple. Terrorism is the resurgence of tribalism, which historically signals impending collapse.

All this being said, my keen sense of disappointment is seeming more like clinical depression. Mankind helplessly driven by irrational forces too primal to expunge? Driven to destroy itself through unmitigated aggression, overpopulation, or both? No, I am not depressed but, like de Chardin, ever the optimist. He recognized that while civilizations rise and fall in a cycle, they seem to return at a higher level of coalescence. They cycle but in an upward spiral. There *are* men of reason, and sometimes we are lucky enough to have them as leaders.

It happened at Runnymede in 1215, when English barons drafted the Magna Carta, for the first time placing limits on the power of the monarch over individual liberty. In the late eighteenth century, the founding fathers of that rebellious English colony, the United States of America, passed a constitution that took account, with unusual realism, of human nature, codifying checks and balances to nullify the inevitable abuses of power. After more sophisticated Europeans gradually subdued the native tribes in the manner of empires before them, the United States became a great melting pot. Other modern democracies seem to have outgrown internal conflicts to become multicultural, though these nations may be regarded as larger tribes. Struggles in postcolonial Africa, where borders were drawn with slight regard for tribal territories, point to the importance of tribal identity to national stability.

Nonetheless, social evolution has brought us a long way toward unification, conquering the dark side of tribal warfare. At this time, the resurgence of tribalism that threatens us stems from the failure of the civilized world to appreciate, understand, and incorporate the positive role of the tribe. To reach the next level of de Chardin's spiral, we need to be realistic about human nature—to acknowledge that it arises from self-replication, the demands of which continue to be irresistible, including the demand for an affiliative group of limited size. Call it something new—Match.com or Facebook—it is the tribe. We also need to keep population growth within the threshold of vital resources, perhaps by shifting more power from the male to the female agenda. It is no coincidence that wherever women have more reproductive rights, population tends to stabilize or decline.

THE FIRST RULE

In a culture now so drenched in sex, why would there be any resistance to a Sexual Theory of Everything? Generations have matured equating love with lovemaking or what was quaintly referred to in more restrained times as "carnal knowledge." Most especially the women seem to have changed to embrace the notion that they are men with different sex organs. They claim the same sexual appetites and the same independent disdain of commitment; they dress like men, drink and talk like men. This is all a cultural aberrancy, fraught with danger to future children.

The modern descent into decadence and licentious behavior is not what I have in mind in proposing this theory. I am not affirming that old wag in implying that sexual activity is so central to human life that we may as well acknowledge it as all-encompassing. My theory goes further to say that self-replication, being the primeval distinction of life itself, resonates through all of human affairs: things we consider free of it, like religion, and things we stubbornly consider rational, like history or politics. Such an idea will threaten the average person who will be thinking, "I am still civilized and completely rational. I do not identify with a tribe or even a racial group. Why, some of my best friends are (insert, for example, black, Jewish, Catholic, Latino), *but I wouldn't want my daughter to marry one.*" That is where I have you, vindicating the first rule: to duplicate oneself as closely as possible.

A classic *Star Trek* episode involved two intergalactic antagonists who are black on one side and white on the other. When the rational Vulcan Mr. Spock asked them why they were fighting to the death since they were each half black and half white, the human, irrational response was, "Don't you see? He is black on the *right* side, while I am black on the *left* side. I am *white* on the right side." The germ cells, agents of the SROCs, drive us to dig for some perceptible distinction, invent one if necessary. In the increasingly difficult attempt to satisfy the first rule of self-replication—ensuring conformity of our descendants—we must define and circumscribe a comfortably small reproductive circle. This invention of differences in itself proves my point about searching for that tribal circle in the mating game. What is so different between the Catholics and Protestants in Ireland or between Jews and Arabs, both Semitic peoples, that they hate one another and refuse to intermarry? The Jews, in their phenomenal ethnic and religious cohesion, are especially emblematic of the extreme negative potential of tribalism, having been historical scapegoats, targeted by a crude nativism we now call anti-Semitism. These feuds take on centuries of bitter history, while their primitive origins are lost in the mists of time.

Neither am I making light of cultural differences. Many a marriage has run aground upon a failure to appreciate their true importance, since to live with someone whose worldview is opposite of one's own may prove impossible. In some cultures, life is considered a curse to be endured; in others, a blessing to be enjoyed. Your daughter may not have fully understood your *rational* concerns about her marriage to a Jew, but if only you had explained how much his people relied for their sustenance on fish—tuna salad, smoked salmon, pickled herring—as opposed to chicken, roast beef, and, (God save you) the most iniquitous, pork!

The fact is we all want to believe that we are rational, that we have things under our conscious control, and that we are not driven by unconscious forces frighteningly beyond the control of reason. We resist the theory of blind irrational forces in spite of clear and abundant evidence that they prevail in all human affairs. The truly *rational* thing would be to face up to irrationality, but our faculty of reason evolved as a means to adapt and survive, and it evolved only so far as needed in meeting that aim while unconscious, often irrational forces are the foundations of life itself.

IN CONCLUSION: CONSCIOUSNESS

Once the ability to replicate had evolved, the processes of natural selection could work to enable the emergence of more sophisticated organisms adapted to the varied and variable environments the earth provided. One of the most useful adaptations was sentience—to see, to hear, and to feel the environment. Along with the sense organs came the nervous system to process this data, and then came the brain, our own specialty, bringing the mysterious faculty of consciousness.

The new frontiers of what is called neuropsychiatry are delving into this most interesting faculty of human consciousness, its distinctive feature being *self*-consciousness. We are set apart from other species by this finely evolved consciousness, giving us the notion of individual selfhood. We see its origins in prehistory when early humanoids first noticed their dead, paying them special attention and homage. Ideas of a soul, spirits, and gods followed. The notion of something inhabiting the body, the *homunculus,* an idea that somehow migrated from medieval alchemy to neuroscience and psychology, is described by neuropsychiatrist Antonio Damasio as Descartes' Error, the title of his excellent book on the subject. The error in our concept, going back to Descartes, is that the mind is separate from the body, when it is evident in patients with brain injury or stroke victims that the mind is the function of the brain.

We are reluctant to believe it, suffering mental blocks in our attempt to think clearly and objectively about our humanity. We do not want to think of our selfhood as merely the result of electrochemical activity or that we are links in an unbroken chain of life, driven by unconscious, irrational forces. We find it unthinkable to consider life as a state of nonlife, since sentience, especially consciousness, stands out in conspicuous contrast to the inanimate. Ultimately life emerged, with all the same materials, from nonlife. With our special brains giving us the seemingly incontrovertible impression that we are each some special, ethereal entity that has entered a bodily shell, how can we find otherwise? We are doing so by using the brain to study the brain and uncover the tricks it plays on us.

It would appear that our clear, objective, scientific thinking about ourselves might lead us into a depressive state and that my theory may suggest that humans are no better than animals that can be forgiven their natures by reason of rudimentary biology. Have I not further implied that our human lives, circumscribed by birth and death, are defined by the meaningless perpetuation of birth and death, nothing more? This is a harsh theory, even if corroborated by science, yet it is increasingly hard for modern people to turn to the supernatural religions that fly in the face of both science *and* reason.

When I joke that Judaism is all about food and Christianity all about sex, friends knowing my Buddhist affinity ask me what Buddhism is all about. An easy question, the reply to which is *reality*. While it gets a bum rap for "navel gazing," Buddhism is about facing reality and, without flinching, discovering its true and hidden nature. Through the gift of our superior consciousness, humans alone have access to intuitions about this nature, helped along by meditative practices. These amazing intuitions, even those we reject as irrational, are vindicated by nuclear physics as it advances our understanding of matter. What is the fundamental particle? If not the atom, then perhaps the subatomic particle, the quark, the string? Deeper and deeper into the essence of matter, substance disappears; it is energy itself, and we have no idea what energy is. Modern science has revealed fascinating aspects of this world and the universe it occupies while leaving us at the abyss of nihilism. Only Buddhism jumps that abyss, and I find there the most profound thought mankind has as yet produced.

A Sexual Theory of Everything describes the long, karmic adventure we know as life on earth. Along with all of modern science, it disappoints our yearning to see ourselves as special and individual. To the secular agnostic, it amplifies the all-too-common "existential angst" of modern life. It is almost easier, and more pleasant, to deal with people of faith who have come to some answers, satisfying to themselves if simplistic to others. One hopes for them that their answers hold up under the extreme grinding of karmic experience, but the faithless ones come to the abyss and stop. Even if as a species we improve our condition, making earthly life more tolerable, one's individual life is finite and therefore seemingly meaningless.

Meaning is not intrinsic to life but rather a thing we find in it or give to it ourselves. In our personal experiences, we have cause to wonder, a need to understand why things are as they are, why reason never seems to prevail in human affairs. The pursuit of such understanding is what has driven science, religion, and philosophy throughout history. Once having studied the thinking of our predecessors, such a pursuit may well be meaningful to each of us.

ON BUDDHISM

- *A Personal Essay* -

Twelve or thirteen of us in the confirmation class sit around a table with Pastor Bley, a stern clergyman. We are at that uncertain, prepubescent stage of life, the gangly transition to adulthood, yet assured by our religious community that we are ready for the decision to commit ourselves to its doctrine. It is a Saturday, and we would each rather be elsewhere, but our generation still respects parental authority. The reverend, clever man that he undoubtedly is, poses a trick question: "Who believes in the devil?" I alone raise my hand bravely, reasoning that if there is a God, there must be a devil. How else to account for evil?

I knew this was the answer for which the pastor was fishing but did not confess that I did not believe in a devil or in a God, for that matter. Their adversarial relationship seemed too simplistic and superstitious. Rebel though I was, I was nevertheless confirmed and went on to attend a Christian university with staunch rules that included compulsory chapel attendance. By my senior year, our class determined that this requirement was an affront to the freedom of individual conscience, and some of us boycotted chapel. We were barred from attending the graduation ceremony as a consequence.

I cite that incident in confirmation class long ago as the beginning of a spiritual quest that later led me to Buddhism, an unusual path for someone not raised in an Eastern milieu—a Christian, in fact, of a Western culture. At a young age, I grew dissatisfied with

Western religions and began a search for more profound beliefs. I sought to find the deepest thought of which mankind had thus far proven capable and began with a mixture of science and philosophy. I read Konrad Lorenz on the new science of animal behavior called ethology. His book *On Aggression* suggests an evolutionary cause, not the devil, for the evils of mankind; the animal instincts that inhibit murder within other social species were lost in human evolution as we gained the greater adaptability of learning. Among others, I read Aldous Huxley, Bertrand Russell, and French philosopher Bertrand de Jouvenel. *The Phenomenon of Man*, a classic by de Chardin, was persuasive concerning his idea that while civilizations rise and fall, they return each time at a higher level, an upward spiral toward greater enlightenment. I read *The Tao of Physics* by Fritjof Capra, describing the amazing similarity between a Taoist outlook on reality and the discoveries of modern nuclear physics.

In 1979, I came upon *Zen Mind, Beginner's Mind* by Shunryu Suzuki, the Japanese Zen master who founded the San Francisco Zen Center. Zen was considered bizarre and somewhat deranged, but I was curious to look into it. Perhaps Buddhism had something to contribute. The book, published only nine years before, was on its way to becoming a Zen classic and for good reason. When I read, "It seems that we die and that we do not die," it was a eureka moment. Of course, the ultimate reality has to be paradoxical, exactly what our deepest intuitions tell us, the ones we dismiss for being illogical. Against all evidence, we feel as though we have always existed and always will, and despite our memory of them, those who are gone are perceived as though they never existed. We observe change but have no sense of time's reality or motion. Illogical as they seem, these intuitions are true, revealing that logic is not ultimate.

At that point, I could no longer wade through the Western philosophers. Their truth, wise though it might be, seemed superficial, plankton bobbing atop a great deep ocean of reality, skimming the surface. I went on to read *The Three Pillars of Zen* by Roshi Philip Kapleau, the only Westerner to survive the harsh training of a Japanese Zen monastery, and I pondered the epigrammatic parables called koans in a collection of them called *Zen Flesh, Zen Bones*, which included the famous Mumonkon or Gateless Gate of thirteenth-century Chinese master Ekai. The mind-bending koans are without doubt exquisitely instructive.

With my tendency to get to the root of matters, I wanted to read the ancient sutras, the recorded words of the Buddha, and thus I hit upon *A Buddhist Bible* compiled by Dwight Goddard. It includes Sanskrit, Chinese, and Tibetan sources with an introduction by Huston Smith, scholar of comparative religion and author of a standard text on the subject, *The Religions of Man*. Even in translation, the offerings in the Goddard tome were inscrutable, yet with repeated readings of favorite sections, the message began to sink in, especially as by that time I had begun to practice meditation. The idea in the practice of observing mental processes to study the nature of mind, and to disentangle it from the distracting web of thought, was a most effective start toward finding ultimate reality.

Buddha spoke of a universal mind, a thing I had always intuited, and of the reality of transcendence that encompasses all perceived dichotomy. He emphasized egolessness and the patient acceptance of it in relation to oneself and others, telling his followers that we have *no self nature of our own,* the inference being that the self nature we claim is not individual but unitary, singular. He was called the Great Physician because he wanted to spare people the terrible pain and grief of clinging to the temporal things of this world that must perish, and from the time of his enlightenment under the Bodhi Tree, he held out to all of us the assurance that we have the ability to free ourselves from ignorance. We can apprehend ultimate reality because it is nothing other than the essence nature we take for granted while misperceiving.

The subject of Buddhism is enormous, and over time, one can accumulate a confounding amount of knowledge about its precepts and long history. Luckily, the Buddha's message was that each of us can and should make the quest for ultimate truth independently, using the blessing of human consciousness in meditation. The great writings of masters throughout the ages are extremely helpful yet are only fingers pointing at what we must turn to see. While the sutras are beautiful and moving, they are not sacred texts like those that burden other religions. Consequently, over the years, while guided by the core Buddhist beliefs, my worldview—my belief system—has taken on a distinctly individual character.

BEYOND SCIENCE AND RELIGION

The question I am often asked by friends or acquaintances learning of my Buddhist leanings is whether these beliefs bring me solace. I find this a telling question that bespeaks the terrible quandary of modern man. People yearn for solace and yet, in a secular and scientific age, can no longer believe in God or the ancient superstitions of Western religion. In the long term, their yearning will not be satisfied with foolish self-deception. I know better than to answer their question, because not one in a million inquisitors will be open to the patently absurd nature of the ultimate reality. Eyes will roll even at the radical discoveries of nuclear physics at the quantum level: an effect preceding a cause, a particle detected in two locations simultaneously or behaving as a wave instead, material reality being insubstantial energy. No less ridiculous are the observations of astrophysics that the universe expanded from an exploding particle, that it goes on infinitely, or that it is not infinite but stops somewhere. Physics tells us something nonetheless important, i.e., that even the so-called real world is not exactly as we perceive it. People will shrug this off because it appears to make no difference to them.

As for solace, the underlying problem, as I see it, is the overwhelming tendency to look for it by running from reality. The reality of this life, even at its most agreeable, is that we age, sicken, and die, generally after having loved ones torn from us by the same process. There is struggle, pain, and grief aplenty—who would not run from that? The conundrum is that we do not escape by running. In contrast to all other doctrines, Buddhism peers into reality—deeply and with a constant gaze. What is revealed will not be acceptable, will not bring solace or liberation until one finds enlightenment, the mission of every Buddhist on his meditation cushion. Consider the alternative: going through life ignoring the inexorable plunge toward oblivion, clinging to material things and people even as they perish, facing the loss of homeostasis, consciousness, and life itself in mortal dread.

Except insofar as all beings, sentient and insentient, are said to be naturally enlightened, I am not enlightened. I would not be trying to express the inexpressible if I were, but I am on the path, and as the Chinese have it, there are "many paths to one goal." I may surmise that there are as many interpretations of Buddhism as there are Buddhists, although certain regions where it is the established religion tend toward orthodoxy, and many a practitioner will swear to the unique authenticity of his particular revelation. I share what I have come to believe through experience in years of meditation, and if it offends the sectarians, I can only cite the sanction of Buddha himself, who encouraged an independent quest.

What is enlightenment? It is not knowledge or intellect. It is an epiphany of the inexpressible truth, which may come in a flash or slowly, like getting wet in a fog. The path to it diverges drastically from the well-worn ruts of the typical life. Cherished axioms collapse: that we are separate persons each with a certain history and that others are likewise individual beings, that we are born in the past and will die in the future, moving with a river of time. These axioms have been embedded in our brains from birth, and they tether us to suffering. Fortunately, they do not withstand close scrutiny. The thin thread that holds each persona together as the being we know is the capacity of memory. Lose that capacity in global amnesia, and you will no longer know who you are. Fall prey to aphasia from a stroke or other pathology, and you may imagine that your left arm belongs to some other person. Queer things happen when the brain malfunctions, as the common condition of senile dementia demonstrates.

The reality of egolessness, the Buddhist term for the deeper truth of identity, should not be that hard to accept, yet it is, because every living thing has the survival instinct. We cling to this individual self, and it can be a long path to the dawning realization that we might best loosen our grip. This precept is sometimes criticized as a kind of defensive depersonalization—hiding from misery by denying selfhood, but there is a line, however fine and subtle, between such a defense mechanism and the true state, which is personal while singular. In actuality, we must break through the defenses of ego, the constant agitation of egoistic concerns, to reveal the true egoless self. All reality then becomes our selfhood: the tops of the trees, the sky, the heavenly bodies, friends, acquaintances, and strangers in the marketplace. The one self is inseparable from the myriad things, unlike the isolated self of the ego. Egolessness is liberating in this way and euphoric.

ON THE PATH

The Buddhist path becomes a way of life, of study and meditation, and thus of slowly becoming freer, wiser. The meditation I practice is a clearing of the mind, allowing rising thoughts to pass unattended while observing that the mind is always present even when not busy with thought, just as each of the sense minds is tuned in, absent of stimuli. Hearing does not disappear, for example, when there is silence. The wonder of these observations is the revelation of fundamental reality, a clarity of mind obscured in ordinary life by superficial chaos and a sense of connection or identity with a universal presence, a universal mind. I believe this connection with the universal mind explains a variety of paranormal phenomena such as precognition, retrogressive memory of former lives, and the so-called out-of-body experience. The universal mind is the font of all potentiality, so that in certain states, we may become open to uncommon, disconcerting knowledge.

Meditation brings an awareness of transcendence, which to me is the essential principal. The ultimate nature of reality cannot be this *or* that; it must encompass all duality. It must harbor light and dark, sound and silence, good and evil. Getting back to the late Pastor Bley: yes, if there is a God, there must be a devil, but then God is not supreme, does not transcend. There has to be something beyond God, beyond the universe. In other words, the dichotomous world of our perceptions is like a hall of mirrors with images bouncing back and forth into infinity. As long as there remains the implication that something must lie *beyond*, we are not observing ultimate reality. The obvious corollary to this principle of transcendence is that the ultimate cannot be observed, because what is observable excludes the observer. Nothing can be outside of the ultimate. It is the Tao; it is *oneness*. The term is much bandied by people who do not understand or who fail to appreciate its true depth, but "oneness" is the only way to describe what is meant by transcendence.

TRUE SELF

In his book *Descartes' Error*, cited in the last essay, author Antonio Damasio describes what he calls a "second order mapping" in the human brain: in effect, an extra layer of consciousness that results in our unique *self*-consciousness. We are not only conscious, we are *conscious* of being conscious. That extra layer may be what Tibetans refer to as our "intrinsic awareness." Consciousness is a tool of the mind that I believe refracts the pure light of transcendent reality, like a prism, into the myriad perceptions we discriminate, including ourselves. My further belief is that our extra layer of consciousness is what creates in us the idea of a special, individual self—an immortal soul—inhabiting the body, when in truth there is no evidence of such a being. The sense of that inner presence may be mistaken for God even by nonreligious people. We are each stamped with a unique character, but the reality is deeper.

The selfhood uncovered in meditation—true self nature—always present under the distracting thought clouds, is not an individual ego but the one Self, which I call the Singularity.

At the same time, we do not err in our everyday lives by affirming the self we know. It is the true self but misperceived as an ego we possess individually. It is the essence of ultimate, transcendent reality, the eye that cannot see itself, the ear that cannot hear itself. To realize that this "small mind" has all along been the *one Mind*, the universal mind shared by all, is to become a "great warrior with a mighty sword." That sword is freedom, especially from fear.

Bearing as they do upon our definition of self, Buddhist precepts and the practice of meditation are particularly relevant to fear. The nature of fear goes from abstraction to reality as the ultimate boundary of self-definition, the body, is breached. Fear takes us inward to the core of what we call "self." Those of us with the great good fortune of health do not normally face real fear until the aging process wears off the veneer of immortality and decrepitude advances. No longer a youngster, I have myself had health scares when cancer might well have been the verdict, and strikingly, though I had been involved in the disease and death of my own parents, dying was still an abstraction until it concerned my own body. This fact introduced the unhappy thought that there may be no way to prepare for such an experience, that disaster must be lived to be appreciated. The ultimate disaster is lived only once, adding urgency to the quest for realization.

Many people harbor two unquestioned illusions about the self: that the mind is the self and that it is somehow trapped in the body. There is nothing in this body; it *is* the mind, it *is* the self. It is our only medium for discerning *what is* and for discovering that we ourselves are *what is*, none other. We are what we experience; we are not beings subjected to experience. We *are* the sickness or health, the pain or the pleasure. Our preferences and attachments—labeling one sensation pleasant and therefore good and another painful and bad—arise from the underlying illusion that we stand apart from ourselves as onlookers, passing judgment on the proceedings. It is that unique extra layer of consciousness leaving a false impression.

Buddha displayed the uncanny insight that we must carry within ourselves an ultimate knowledge of the reality of which we are part and that this subjective knowledge is not of the codifiable, intellectual sort but of the nature of profound and inexpressible revelation. I will go further, and here I invoke the sensibility of all those people who report feeling the presence of God within themselves. I believe that our intuition detects the character of the Singularity, the one transcendent Self, in it discerning three traits: wisdom, strength, and compassion. This belief may reflect my Christian upbringing, yet these qualities are those applied to God and evidenced by saints of every faith. Collectively and individually, we find reality to be benign, and like Anne Frank, even in the worst of circumstance, we see a basic goodness in people.

KARMA, TIMELESSNESS, AND TRANSCENDENCE

In common with other Asian religions, a foundational aspect of Buddhist thought is the concept of karma: the principle that everything we perceive and experience in this world—the sangsara as it is referred to in contrast to nirvana[1]—is the effect of cause. With honest reflection, this principle is true yet unacceptable in its broader implications. Simple things are easy to see: seasonal weather variation is caused by the planet's revolution around the sun and local conditions by the movement of air masses. The effect of coronary disease will cause chest pain and shortness of breath. Applied to human behavior, it becomes another matter. For example, every person alive is the product of his genetic inheritance

---

1. Also transliterated "samsara." I take this version from Dwight Goddard's compilation *A Buddhist Bible*. Upon his enlightenment, Tibetan saint Milarepa is said to have declared, "Nirvana and sangsara are dependent and relative states issuing from the void."

affected by his culture and family nurturance, even criminals and psychopaths. People without conscience are the terrible effect of invidious cause; evil is karmic. Such examples are only observations, but they offend the human sense of justice, which we should note has no parallel in nature. We need to believe there is some agency, some culpable devil against whom to satisfy our hunger for vengeance. Unfortunately, the stark reality is just cause and effect.

The linchpin holding together these Buddhist principles is a reality that is next to impossible for us to imagine, let alone embrace: timelessness. While damnably illogical, intuition informs us that our perception of time is an illusion created as we observe change. Despite its seemingly undeniable existence and the shackles of language that bind us to the idea of it, I have always sensed the unreality of time. As far as I know, there is only that British physicist, Julian Barbour, who shares my disbelief. His book, *The End of Time,* harks back to contemporaries of Newton who took issue with his neglect of fundamentals, assuming without deeper examination the existence of space and time. Barbour sets about proposing a quantum cosmology based on the ideas of Newton's rivals such as Leibniz and Descartes, including the notion of a static and timeless universe where motion is only our observance of successive instants, which Barbour calls "nows." He writes, "Such configurations, which can be fabulously richly structured, are the ultimate things. There are infinitely many of them" (Barbour 2001, 16).

These instants of time may be compared to the frames of a motion picture, each one changing minutely as they pass in sequence. The universe of omnipotentiality, all the past, present, and future potential, are there contained in timelessness.

Barbour goes on to discuss Einstein's equations, which become problematic in light of advances in the understanding of quantum mechanics. Eliminate time as a function, and the problems disappear. I observed the unlikely fact of a vector—time—that moves in only one direction with a motion I cannot say I have ever felt. We witness things changing at varying rates, and we invent a measure of these rates, calling it "time." Even the tool we use to quantify this conceit is seen to change in a predetermined way: the hands of the clock change position, and on that basis, we say that something called *time* has passed. I did not feel it. Did you?

The transcendent oneness that is the ultimate nature of reality, encompassing all the dual realm we perceive along with our self nature, is timeless—not mortal, not immortal, but timeless. As hard as it is to believe, timelessness is a requirement for all the other precepts I have described to be true. These are true, as absurd as they may seem, because all other options are still more absurd: a supreme being, creator of all things, who remains aloof from his creation; a universe, incomprehensibly vast, sprinkled throughout with fiery balls visible in our night sky; the desperate meaninglessness of life.

The things to which we cling—a certain self, the world we know through our five senses—are not what they seem. The ultimate nature of these forms is emptiness. This term as used in Buddhism is another that is interpreted differently by each person and therefore widely misunderstood. It is confused with a nihilism more aptly associated with modern science that finds, in the final analysis, no substantiality in matter. Upon his enlightenment, Buddha is said to have declared, "All things are tathagata," meaning that all things come forth from the Void, which is also referred to as the Womb of Tathagata. This void is not empty. The confusion arises in the failure to see the paradox created by transcendence. That form is emptiness means that emptiness equates to form. Both are aspects of oneness and thus are transcended along with all dichotomies in the dual realm. Consider the yin-yang symbol, the perfect emblem of duality; in the background, overlooked, is the circle containing these polarities. They are ultimately encompassed as one, transcended, and thus, in defiance of logic, not mutually exclusive.

Another metaphor for transcendence is the view of Earth from outer space. Rooted to the surface by the amazing force of gravity, we perceive the light of day alternately with the dark of night.

Rise high enough to see the planet as a whole, and it is one globe, lighted on one side and dark on the other. In like manner for all the dichotomies we experience, their poles are two sides of one thing.

The all-encompassing oneness has the essence of void or emptiness, which is, as I said, refracted through the prism of human consciousness into perceptible forms including the true self. To gain this perspective on selfhood, at one with all things, is to be free of fear and grief. We cling to temporal things even as they perish, when in truth there is no one to cling and nothing to cling to.

STEEPING IN THE TIMELESS MIND

What difference does any of this make? How does it aid us in navigating the treacherous shoals of karmic existence? We still must deal with life, make our way through its phases, as time—real or not—seems to pass. This is where meditation enters in, and it is a lifelong process. My practice is not contemplation or "mindfulness" as that is currently understood, which is a focus on the present moment. Neither is it "still sitting." There is an element of discipline to it but not control. One cannot order the mind to stop thinking, yet to observe how each train of thought arises, how it will invariably produce some degree of muscle tension, then to relax and let the train go past, produces a mental state that is quiet but still alert. This is the clear mind, as still as a pool in a grotto. When the neurochemical waves in the brain have been allowed to settle, we experience timelessness where past, present, and future have no meaning and there is no ego self trapped in a temporal delusion. Timelessness, the ultimate nature of reality, thus may be said to explode one's karmic fate—there is no river of time, no continuous persona. Karma does not change; no *deus ex machina* comes down to intervene in our fate, but the change in our perspective makes all the difference.

I think of my meditation as steeping in this timeless state of mind. I believe it creates a growing equanimity, what Suzuki called "imperturbable composure," brought about by nondiscrimination, which is the last tenet I include in this brief *apologia pro vita sua*. We reflexively judge circumstances as good or bad when in reality they come about through causes and conditions. Good conditions are one thing, bringing happiness, but circumstances we perceive as difficult or painful may be irremediable and require our acceptance. To suspend judgment or discrimination permits us to countenance the "moon face" of Buddha along with his sun face. We do not escape karma, but with intrinsic awareness, we glimpse the mind, the transcendent Singularity, that is our true essence. This mind belongs to no one: not to us individually, not to God in heaven.

Thirty-six years after my introduction to the profound doctrines of Buddhism, I published *Conjuring Archangel: Chronicle of a Journey on the Path*, a work of creative nonfiction, imagined as a nightly dialogue between a woman and her spirit guide, Archangel, whom she conjures at an especially difficult time in her life. In the process of steering her on the true path of Buddhism, he explicates its precepts and, through his teaching, the evolution of my ideas on the subject. Any attempt to write about Buddhism is fraught, because language itself is what shackles us to ignorance, while the precepts of this faith are inexpressible. Buddha's famous Lotus Sermon, which disappointed an expectant crowd of disciples, had him sitting silently contemplating a lotus blossom. Only Mahakasyapa understood the wordless meaning, leading him to be seen as the father of Zen.

The publication of *Conjuring Archangel* in 2015 was my primary goal upon retiring. Aware as I had been of the spiritual hunger abroad in the wasteland between cold science on the one hand and the implausible superstitions of religion on the other, I wanted to offer to earnest seekers a roadmap to ultimate reality, which is "of the mind itself."

Cultivate this mind, observe and learn, and then join Omar Khayyam, the ancient Persian poet, who was able to enjoin:

While the rose blows along the river brink,
With old Khayyam the ruby vintage drink,
And when the Angel with his darker draught draws up to thee,
Take that and do not shrink! (Fitzgerald 1952, 65)

DECLINE AND FALL

- *The Tribal Mindset* -

Sir Arthur Conan Doyle acquired his gift for storytelling at the knee of his Irish mother whose interest in English history, especially the old days of chivalry, her son shared. He considered his historical novels, such as *The White Company*, superior to his most popular and profitable Sherlock Holmes mysteries. The following excerpt from his short story, "The Last of the Legions," published in 1905 and still available online, aptly illustrates the fate of the British Isles and of Europe as the Roman Empire frayed around the edges, withdrawing to Rome and loosing the primitive tribes on each other.

> Licinius Crassus, the head of the British military establishment, was a large, bearded man in a white civilian toga, hemmed with the Patrician purple. His rough, bold features…were shadowed with anxiety as he looked with questioning eyes at the drawn, haggard face of the viceroy.
>
> "I fear, your excellency, that you have had bad news from Rome."
>
> "The worst, Crassus. It is all over with Britain…The old German hive is about to swarm once more. There are fresh crowds of Barbarians from Dacia and Scythia. Every sword is needed to hold the Alpine passes. They cannot let three legions lie idle in Britain…"

> "My God, what will be the end of these poor Britons! From ocean to ocean there is not a tribe which will not be at the throat of its neighbor when the last Roman…has turned his back."

Often dominating the daily news today is Afghanistan, which has for centuries proven to be a stubborn throwback to prehistoric human society—in other words, a tribal region. In the *New York Times* of 17 July, 2021, reporters Thomas Gibbons-Neff and Najim Rahim wrote:

> Concerned by the Taliban's offensive, regional power brokers are again recruiting and arming volunteer militias. But some fear the quick fix will lead to a wider breakdown…Omid Wahidi was born after the United States invaded Afghanistan in 2001. His childhood, for the most part, was peaceful. His family farmed eggplant, tomato and okra in the country's north…Mr. Wahidi, with his slight frame and mop of brown hair, carries an assault rifle now…one of many Afghans who have been swept up in a militia recruitment drive…These militias are not new, and have carried many names in the past two decades, often under the auspices of government ownership: local police, territorial army, popular uprising forces, pro-government militias and so on.

In other words, they are tribes. There can be no argument that humans are social animals. Human tribes are scarcely different from packs of dogs, not in relative size nor in behavior and with the notable exception that unlike dogs, humans are capable of killing their own. As primates, our tribal nature has come down to us from our prehistoric ancestors, including early protohumans from whom we diverged millions of years ago. To examine the tribal pattern we inherit, we ought first to look at our close primate relatives. In some ways, human tribes are similar, and in others they differ. Among other primates, unlike most human tribes, kinship groups are matrilineal. Chimpanzees, for example, maintain close ties with the mother, and rhesus macaques bond with one another based on descent from the same female. Similar to humans, patterns of social organization are various from polygamous gibbons to monogamous gorillas. Size of group varies as well as interaction between groups. Forest-dwelling gorillas and orangutans keep to themselves, while our close cousin the chimp is aggressively territorial, presaging our capacity for violence.

Advancing far beyond primate relatives with our unique human endowments—the opposable thumb, upright posture, and articulate tongue—early tribes banded together to trade with their neighbors or conquer them, forming ever-larger societies and eventually civilizations. Human history from ancient times is a catalog of these empires rising and falling on every continent. The cause of their seemingly inevitable collapse is the subject of conjecture among historians, but the aftermath is the relapse to tribes.

The largest and arguably the most influential empire in the Western world was Rome, and its fall from the fourth to the fifth century was cataclysmic. The loss of political unity and military control was gradual, but eventually the empire was overwhelmed by barbarian groups, among them Huns, Goths, Vandals, and Visigoths. In Britain, the sixth-century monk Gildas wrote, "The barbarians drive us to the sea; the sea throws us back on the barbarians. Thus two modes of death await us, we are either slain or drowned."[2] The Romans could not assist them. Even aside from invasions from without, the Romans themselves descended into civil wars, often enlisting barbarian tribal warriors in the violence.

Concerning the fall of Rome, historian Glen Bowersock writes, "It has been valued as an archetype for every perceived decline, and

---

2. Wikipedia: Fall of the Western Roman Empire. (Gildas, On The Ruin of Britain (De Excidio Britanniae). gutenberg.org pg. 1949.)

hence for a symbol of our own fears."[3] In Jungian psychology, the term "archetype" is used for a primitive mental image, inherited from the earliest human ancestors and supposed to be present in the collective unconscious. While Rome may represent the paradigm for the collapse of human civilizations throughout history, an archetype in the human psyche is, in my view, the root cause of these failures: the tribal mindset.

The foundation of tribal instincts is an underlying attitude, a presumption, that people who are like me are good and trustworthy, while those who are not are inferior and suspect. This prejudice is easily stoked, as every tyrant knows well, with appeals to communal fears or tribal allegiance, especially where differences between tribes are greatest or most obvious. When tribes coalesce into larger societies, there remains an inherent tension between the tribal and the emerging civilized culture, even more so when one has conquered the other. As generations pass—centuries, in the case of Rome—this tension is suppressed; the tribal mindset burns low on the back burner. Any flickering of it in young minds is suspected of having been inculcated by backward parents, never considered a natural trait.

A lyric in "You've Got to Be Carefully Taught," a song from the 1949 musical *South Pacific,* score by Richard Rodgers and words by Oscar Hammerstein, sums up the idea:

> You've got to be taught
> Before it's too late,
> Before you are six or seven or eight,
> To hate all the people your relatives hate.
> You've got to be carefully taught.

It is a fine, idealistic notion that we might see the end of schoolyard bullies or eliminate all social conflict by improving our educational

---

3. Wikipedia: Fall of the Western Roman Empire. (Glen Bowersock, "The Vanishing Paradigm of the Fall of Rome" *Bulletin of the American Academy of Arts and Sciences* 1996. vol. 49 no. 8 pp. 29–43.)

and parenting methods. Yet we each have personal experience of the tribal as children on the playground: the loneliness, the gathering in small cliques, the sense of security and belonging, and the conformity enforced by the need to be accepted even if conformity involves cruelty to others. Any teacher at a primary school will know that children are not taught bias; they are taught tolerance. The fact that clannish attitudes of "us versus them" are passed down in families is evidence that the tribal mindset still burns, however low, in the most civilized of societies, and since the history of civilization is but a fraction of the span of time that mankind has lived in tribes, that mindset is unlikely to be stamped out. How does this underpinning of tribalism, smoldering so long, come eventually to flare up and overcome a great civilization?

Civilization holds the seeds of its own destruction, and unfortunately, we are witness to their germination in our own time with America being the hothouse where best to see them sprout. A successful democracy, unassailable economy, home of the free and the brave, when on 5 November, 2016, the nation and the world awoke to the shocking revelation that Donald Trump had been elected the American president, laying bare a schism that had been cleaving the population for years. How could a firebrand, anti-immigrant populist, elevated with a minority of the votes, now lead a country once known as the "melting pot," a place where people from foreign lands were welcomed and where they in turn celebrated the opportunity to become American?

The definition of *melt* is "to disappear as if by dissolving, to lose outline or distinctness, blend." Its antonym means "to emerge, break out." Before we leave the dictionary, I would point to the synonyms *irony* and *paradox,* both of which describe the contradiction or internal inconsistency we see in the United States as I write. It is a process we might call "reverse melting," and it is *paradoxical* at a time when the 2020 census shows more people of mixed race than ever before. *Ironically,* even as the population blends, we witness each minority *emerge* and *break out* from that melting pot to assert their pride of culture and history, seek political power, and raise money for their own particular museum—on the national Mall, of course. Partisans engage in identity politics using buzzwords on the left like "inclusiveness" and "diversity" and dog whistles on the right such as "border security," "election integrity," and the perennial "law and order." With no vision of the end result, what is emerging is the tribal mindset, the seed of our coming destruction—sooner or later.

America is not alone in the development; the descent is global, as Afghanistan and its neighbors can attest. Autocrats are emboldened in Ukraine, Belarus, Russia, and China, to name but a few, while liberal democracy, constituting the essence of modern civilization, fades in influence. In each case, the tyrant represents one tribe intent upon dominating all the others. There ensues an era of violent purging, the desperate flight of large numbers, and the gathering resistance of rival tribes that go underground where tribal war resumes.

The cracks in a civilization begin to show when after many, even innumerable, generations, one takes its blessings so entirely for granted that it feels free to criticize them, and there is always a good deal of fault to find. Historically, the rise of a civilization has involved conquest: one powerful tribe over others or over foreign lands and the enslavement of their people. Native societies, their culture and languages, are stifled, whole tribes killed off by a novel disease like smallpox in the Americas. The violence and cruelty of conquest is rightly decried, as it came to be in the Age of Enlightenment. By the seventeenth and eighteenth centuries, Western philosophy, denouncing the evils of civilization, offered in contrast the idea of "the noble savage," which became a stock phrase after first appearing in a play by John Dryden in 1672. No less of a social critic than the celebrated and highly opinionated author, Charles Dickens contributed a scathing piece, intensely sarcastic of the sentimental notion, "The Noble Savage," to his magazine *Household Words* in 1853.

We need not go that far back to hear the more recent and much louder cries within civilized societies against the wickedness of imperialism from people who romanticize primitive mankind and his tribal existence. For a reality check on tribal barbarism, if you have a strong stomach, look at Frederick W. Hodges' *Handbook of the American Indians* and find an excruciating description of the ritual tortures that customarily awaited captives of the enemy tribes, even before the arrival of Europeans. Some tribes were not as brutally cruel; in the eastern Woodlands and southern Canada, captives would be adopted or sold into slavery. On the Northwest coast, enslaved captives could be used as gifts in potlatch ceremonies.

Is tribal life itself a Hobbesian "state of nature" and the life of the primitive tribesman "solitary, poor, nasty, brutish, and short"? Surely not solitary nor necessarily poor, nasty, or brutish but short for certain. There are distinct advantages to tribal life that, added to its inherence in human nature, must account for its tenacity. The modest size of a tribe relative to a modern nation, for example, and its foundation in kinship provide the security of cohesion, including a comfortable pool of potential mates. The stability of familiar customs gives men positions in the community—warriors, shamans, hunters—and women as gatherers and later the first to till the soil.

The ancient Hebrew tribes, and even their modern-day descendants, represent the strongest, most enduring example of tribal benefits, preserving religious and dietary laws through many millennia. Arguably, this strict adherence may have triggered the xenophobia that gave rise to anti-Semitism, though many Jews will disagree vehemently. By no means do I blame the victims for this persistent, irrational prejudice, yet one cannot deny the irony that a fortress mentality has buttressed their solidarity throughout the ages.

If kinship was the cement of tribal life, religion has been the sand and gravel that hold tribesmen in concrete. In human evolution, the animal instincts, including the inhibition against killing one's own kind, faded through natural selection in favor of a capacity to learn and thereby adapt to changes in the environment. Loosed from instinct, an individual's behavior was controlled by the tribal society, thanks to the remaining foundational trait of human nature as a social species, and religion dictated the rules, rituals, and beliefs. Religion determined what was proper, what was immoral or evil, and when it was right to kill and when not. The dark side of this tribal order was and is an oppressive, stultifying conformity and the destructive ability to incite bias and violence against the next tribe or any nonbelievers.

Tribal customs may vary widely from the humane to the barbaric. Loyalty to and sharing with other tribe members, caring for one another through hard times, and a sense of belonging define the positive, humane aspects of tribal life. Contrariwise, on the warpath, the tribe gives permission to kill, or in some machismo tribes, it may be righteous to kill an adulterous wife or sinful daughter. A heretic could be subject to any of the most hideous forms of execution such as beheading or burning at the stake. Rising civilizations might retain much barbarism and even invent new forms. The Romans practiced mass crucifixions to terrorize conquered tribes as the empire expanded, but the French thought of the guillotine as a more merciful way to put people to death. As civilization is an amalgam of tribes, laws cannot correspond perfectly with differing tribal customs, yet eventually a majority must recognize and accept some form of justice.

Over time, the justice system and the tangle of legal codes become strangling, and there can be no doubt that tribal cohesion is slowly lost along with esprit de corps, the security of belonging to the group, knowing how to behave, and confidence in loyalty and support. Fear, insecurity, frustration, and anger arise, and at some point the instinctive tribal mindset comes to the fore. Today, the germinating seeds of destruction enjoy a climate of exponential population growth. Modern civilization is collapsing under the weight of more than *seven billion* human beings.

As the maelstrom swirls violently around us, we struggle in furious desperation to find answers, routes of escape, processes to employ, and policies to enact. We puzzle and wonder as our fevered brains come up blank. Climate change? Too late; the planet is a greenhouse and in many places is rapidly becoming uninhabitable. A global pandemic? How many will die before we can vaccinate enough people? Birth control? No, by no means! Read my first essay. The forces of nature will not be subdued. Sufficient carbon dioxide in the atmosphere, and the planet becomes a greenhouse. *Homo sapiens* crowding cheek by jowl into spaces occupied by wild animals, and a mutant microbe leaps at the opportunity to infect a susceptible species. In the face of these escalating crises, the ultra-wealthy appear to have latched onto the heavenly bodies as a possible refuge. A far out idea, literally, yet they forge ahead with it, building their private space ships. Governments struggle to enact laws or policies to encourage environmental friendliness or promote new ways to mitigate looming consequences: build dikes, windmills, solar panels, and electric cars, desalinate sea water, and on and on. The tribes push back, because the force of our own nature, especially the tribal mindset, is equally as indomitable as all others.

The seeds of destruction have been sprouting for some time, at least a generation, so that we may begin to identify the tendrils. Noticeable has been geographical segregation into tribal regions according to race, religion, politics, and economic class, and these regions are tending to become more homogeneous. Wealthy, right-wing Christians will live in certain neighborhoods and often gravitate to places harboring their tribe, now known in America as "red states." The right wing is openly tribal in recent years, abandoning all pretension to the contrary. Unfortunately, their tribe includes much of the working class, poorly educated and living in remote areas without connection to the modern world. The polar opposite tribe is the left wing: young, highly diverse urban dwellers who continue to dissemble with respect to their tribal nature. As time goes by, the true picture comes into focus. They are the "politically correct" tribe, obsessed with conformity to groupthink and adherence to conventions of culture, dress, music, and media. Distinctions between tribes have become so obvious that a postal code reveals an individual's tribal membership, how he votes, and what radio station he prefers.

The urban tribe is the more humane and continues to uphold the liberal democracy that has long been the dearest blossom of modern civilization. Being young and naive, these urbanites fail to appreciate the powerful forces against them. Clustered into cities, any power they might exercise is reduced, especially in the United States, given its stubbornly obsolete election laws. The many-faceted diversity of the urban tribe has the potential to undermine whatever cohesion it presently enjoys. Diverse minority groups that have *broken out* and *emerged* from the melting pot might in future split into smaller tribes: black versus white, gay versus straight, native born versus immigrant. Choose your side. At present, these benighted children seem to believe that the best way to push the wheels of government is not by voting but to protest in the streets, which avails them nothing. They make their wishes known but to less effect than a toddler throwing a tantrum. Before the babes grow up, the wealthy and powerful tribe will have seized total control of their lives. That is when they will cleave; they will revert to type. Under pressure, the innate tribal mindset becomes a matter of *me and mine*.

More civilized people will disown any implication of a tribal mindset, but it is there, often reflective of childhood religious training. A nonreligious Jew will bristle every December at the popularity of the Christmas holiday even though it marks the birth of an ancient Jewish rabbi. A lapsed Catholic will exhibit compulsive behaviors inculcated with the doctrine of original sin, zealously scrubbing the house, face, or teeth. There will be no doubt which tribe they will join when the final bell tolls.

As in the prescient words of T. S. Elliot, the world ends "not with a bang but a whimper." Decay is slow, whether of infrastructure or of institutions. It took two hundred chaotic years of decline for Rome to fall, but the operative number now is seven billion. The crowding together of still more billions onto land masses shrunken by rising seas may of itself halt population growth. The process may already have begun. It will remain for those surviving to die off from plague, fire, flood, extreme heat, or tribal warfare. *Homo sapiens* is not exempt from extinction.

BREEDING

- Know the Dog -

I am dipping a cold toe into the seething ocean of hostile discourse in daring to address the topic of breeding, which, in these days of fractured politics and angry backlash, is increasingly associated with racism and doctrines of white supremacy. I must beg your trust and indulgence for this attempt, as I would dearly love to bring some reason to the fevered subject. Surely we are best cooler from brow to toe.

In modern times, when we think of breeding, we think of animals: cattle and poultry selectively bred for fast growth and other desired qualities, other animals for traits we fancy, even to the detriment of the creature such as thoroughbred horses with spindly legs and bulldogs and Persian cats with pug noses. Especially in our closest companion, the dog, we recognize that specific behaviors and temperaments may be associated with a given breed. Certain hounds have been bred for hunting: the border collie for herding sheep and the bloodhound for tracking a scent. Some breeds are notoriously aggressive, like the shar-pei, a fighting dog in ancient China and favorite pet of emperors, while others like the golden lab are good with children. We are willing to accept that selective breeding over time has produced these consistent results. Know the breed, know the dog.

Breeding was once acceptably applied to humans in a similar sense. The term referred to an individual's family heritage. If he was a royal or an aristocrat, he had good breeding and was expected to be of good character and intelligence. A person from the servant class was not considered well bred. Unlike animals, people have not been deliberately selected for breeding except in the rare irruption of eugenics, yet the attitude persists that personality, temperament, and moral caliber are determined by class. Not surprisingly, this leads to a stubborn rigidity of the social structure, since individuals will be expected to marry one of similar status. In consequence, people of lower status are held back, their abilities, which in some cases may be considerable, going unrecognized, while those royals and aristocrats may not be as uniformly estimable as advertised.

There is a certain loss of social capital, but for better or worse, the stratification of social classes can be seen as self-perpetuating. People will be shaped by their early experiences, and the lower strata will have fewer opportunities than the upper class. At each level, they will develop as they are allowed, for the most part accepting the status quo. For centuries, the ruling classes throughout the civilized world held to power and wealth, while those on the lower rungs lived another reality, downstairs of their employers or masters where they had their own hierarchy. The butler and the housekeeper were above the maids and the footmen; the house slaves, above the field hands. In some cases, the laborers were not only willing but worshipful of a godlike ruler as, for example, the serfs who built the splendid palaces of the Russian czar.

The preponderance of people would not have labored at the castle but would be poor, struggling, and taxed while otherwise removed from consideration. There might be resentment and occasionally revolution, but such conflicts would change only the face of the ruler, not the perquisites everyone accepted as his. The impoverished multitudes were not evident in history books or literature unless to be mocked as the jesters or dolts: Bottom, the weaver in *A Midsummer Night's Dream,* whose head is turned into that of a donkey, and Elbow, a simple constable in *Measure for Measure.* In the nineteenth century, some social conscience began to take root, with Charles Dickens depicting so effectively the dire circumstances of the lower class in England, and in France, where violence was apt to erupt, Victor Hugo's *Les Miserables*. As another century approached, along with the Industrial Revolution, reformers embraced progressive ideas; movements arose to bring social justice and equality, to erase poverty and class distinctions, thereby improving the human condition, especially for the underprivileged.

    The Great War ushered in the horrific destructiveness of modern combat and ended with such a punitive treaty that wise old heads, including Churchill, foresaw that it was not over at all. Sure enough, before two decades had passed, the world was at war with Hitler's Germany. World War II was an existential conflict and thus enormously expensive. The victorious nations incurred huge debt, and taxation to pay it off was confiscatory. The old wealth, the large estates, were sacrificed. In Britain, a fortunate few properties landed in the National Historic Trust so that tourists may now rent a room where the peerage had held court for generations. The era of rigid social stratification was ended. Butlers and lady's maids were thrown on the job market along with their aristocratic former employers.

    The remainder of the twentieth century was egalitarian, the prevailing wisdom being that individual advancement should no longer be based on birth but on merit. In the United States, the Scholastic Aptitude Test, replacing the patronage of wealth and family connection as the standard for admission to universities, fostered a new meritocracy. All men—and women—would be considered equal, and equality came to mean sameness. Breeding as a criterion for assessing people fell out of favor along with traditional gender roles.

    Social conditions have been improved by these and other modern developments. Open societies give opportunity to people of all stripes, benefitting from their labor and ingenuity. Globalism shrinks the world so that contacts between different cultures can bring understanding as well as goods. More radical than anything in history has been the technology of the internet, an extraordinary means of connecting all kinds of people as never before.

In the course of these enormous changes, the idea that personal characteristics might have some basis in heritage—genetic or cultural—has become offensive. People are mongrels anyway: Do I take after my Irish mother or my German father? Yet the reality of breeding can be clear even in mongrels. A dog of mixed breed will usually have one strain predominate, so that he looks and behaves like a collie, spaniel, or shepherd, and though information concerning individual breeding is not wholly reliable, it can be useful. If a case can be made that the Doberman or pit bull tends toward aggressive behavior, a dog with that heritage should be handled with caution. This aspect of breeding is true of humans as well, though the proposition runs afoul of our orthodoxy regarding cultural stereotypes. In these politically correct times, we dare not suggest that my German father was compulsive in his orderliness or that my mother had an Irish temper. We can, ironically, observe that my brother resembles my mother and inherited her weight problem while I take after my father in appearance. Our thinking on this matter is unintegrated, dichotomous. It is one thing to point out observable physical features that are inherited and another to discriminate personality traits.

Numerous studies of twins are pertinent in showing a biological basis for personality. Identical twins, sharing one hundred percent of their DNA, are observed to have more personality traits in common than fraternal twins, who have only half of the same genes. At the same time, there is anecdotal evidence of a Jekyll and Hyde phenomenon in some twins, each seeming to express opposite sides of one personality—a dominant, aggressive twin paired with his shy and introverted sibling. It is implausible that this phenomenon could result from nurture.

While it may be objectionable to discriminate personality traits in people, we do it and always have. We sometimes generalize extravagantly, creating unflattering caricatures that Poles are inherently stupid, that Jews, Swedes, and Chinese are stingy, that people of Spanish descent are hotheaded, and that black people are lazy. There may be a grain of truth to such characterizations, but it is insufficient to judge individuals who should be free to demonstrate their distinctiveness. In what cases might we consider that the grain of shared, ancient wisdom could be constructive?

I admit to being a booster for marriage of all sorts between races or religions. In causing future generations to blend in physical appearance, interracial marriage would result in less discrimination, and in the passion of youth, religious differences can be overcome, also leading to more tolerance in the world. Too often, given enough time, that grain of ancestral wisdom bearing upon our genetic or cultural differences becomes the intolerable irritant—the pebble in the shoe, the pea under the mattress—especially in time of trouble when a couple might otherwise be pulling together. A good matchmaker, in the past, would look not just at personality but also a person's breeding; it is a realistic consideration whenever two people contemplate serious commitment.

Dissimilarities look small to lovers, but over the course of years in a mixed marriage, they become associated with the alien race, the foreign culture, and hostility brews along with doubts. "He is tuna salad, I am chicken salad! What was I thinking?" Each spouse or both may grow increasingly chauvinistic as hostility rises and attitudes of cultural superiority harden. Such deep conflicts and divisions make it harder to avoid divorce, which is common enough without them.

Some realistic thought about breeding at the start of a relationship might be wise and later prove invaluable. These considerations can be subtle: What psychic baggage comes with a person from a lower economic class or a higher one? What expectations? Might a person with Latin antecedents tend to be emotional? Could some Scandinavian blood make for a shy or taciturn person? The harder part of the assessment is determining to what extent differences will be tolerable or negotiable, since matters related to breeding are easily discounted in the throes of physical attraction.

One must hesitate to broach this subject, as I said, for fear of opening a Pandora's Box of cultural bias and racial discrimination. Our modern era is unparalleled in avoiding open consideration of it in stark contrast to former times. Watch any of the period dramas on *Masterpiece Theatre* for the perfect depiction of the days when breeding was coin of the realm—no bones about it. America, the great melting pot, led the way in discrediting class distinction. According to J. D. Vance in his best-selling memoir *A Hillbilly Elegy*, even there, affirmative action aside, one's social class is a subliminal factor in success. A self-described hillbilly from the mountains of Kentucky, he became a successful attorney thanks to luck, grit, and the Marine Corps and despite the deprivations of a dysfunctional family riven by drug abuse, domestic violence, and divorce. His descriptions of attempting to fit in at Yale Law School show the implicit role of class. In a profession where networking is vital, a familiarity with upper-class conventions is assumed: the etiquette of silverware, a knowledge of wines, what is an appropriate suit for a formal dinner and where to find one. Thanks to his girlfriend, whom he went on to marry, he passed these surprise, unofficial exams.

However unwittingly, people assess one another through the cultural qualities we evince, and I would suggest that this source of information, while potentially unjust in the individual case, may contribute to more realistic views. Consider the job interview, which can be susceptible to unfair bias. We expect positions to be filled by qualified applicants, irrespective of race or ethnicity and even despite piercings and tattoos. We want to think that any person, regardless of background, should have the chance to beat whatever the odds against him. If you are the kind employer offering that chance, you would need to understand and prepare for the challenges and use common sense. A law firm in New York or London might not be the right fit for a new hire from Appalachia raised by a drug-addicted mother who was in and out of jail.

Sensitivity surrounding discussion of breeding correlates with political correctness, the modern movement to promulgate language and policies with the worthy intent, on moral grounds, of avoiding offense or discrimination against disadvantaged segments of society. To raise any concern related to personal background or origin, particularly of an individual belonging to an underprivileged group, is now viewed by society as anathema. Like many a well-intended movement, this one went to an extreme sufficient enough to draw ridicule, with the result that the term "political correctness" is mostly used pejoratively or in satire. In the ongoing culture wars, a backlash has arisen against it.

In the fury of those wars, we lose perspective. Insensitive remarks are repudiated by polite society, and most fair-minded citizens want others to be treated justly, judged only by the "content of their character," in the immortal words of Dr. Martin Luther King Jr. The problem is that there are real differences between people and groups of people. We can be color-blind with respect to equal treatment while still recognizing that reality. We can be accepting of a daughter's relationship with a man of a different race or religion and yet worry whether she knows how his personality has been molded by membership in a persecuted minority or, for that matter, a country club. A good deal of unhappiness in the world is caused by a refusal to give attention to the often-subtle signs of breeding.

It is difficult today to understand that one is not compelled to weigh the relative worth of any obvious distinction, that to note a difference need not signal implicit bias. Some people, perhaps most, may have this judgmental reflex, but if we are *well bred*, we can notice a person's skin color without feeling inferior or superior. Distinctions exist, and it behooves us to know their possible ramifications in order to assess their meaning for us personally. In this process, we apply an individual standard of what we define as good breeding. With animals, a definition is not problematic: a well-bred steer will mature quickly and yield good-quality meat; a well-bred sheep will have fine fleece; a well-bred race horse will come from proven stock. Winning horses can be hired out to stud for large sums. The best-bred border collie will excel at herding ungulates; the best-bred guard dog will be strong and obedient.

With our fellow humans, we may acknowledge some commonality of values: a person who is well bred will be courteous, clean, properly clothed, humble, generous, and reasonably articulate. As we add to this list, we close on the particular definition of our own tribe, and the further we go, the more laughable it grows. No doubt my German father would insist that no person of good breeding would go to bed leaving dirty dishes in the sink, while my Irish mother might add that a well-bred man drinks his Jameson neat. She would go on to observe, "To each his own!" Of late there seems to be no one left who is that tolerant.

Tribalism is the danger, the strong tendency in human nature to lapse into the prehistoric pattern of small, warring kinship groups. Ironically, while the politically correct abhor any consideration of breeding as prejudicial, many others believe that the open discussion of racial and ethnic differences *increases* tolerance. In either case, we should worry about the unintended consequences or antithetical results. Will the backlash of the white male continue to erode the veneer of civilization as it appears to be doing in recent years? At what point do the grievances of minorities, however righteous, erupt in tribal violence?

Preposterous as it seems, only scant provocation has ever been needed to loose the dogs of war and have the "chicken salad" tribe set upon the "tuna salad" people. I am again reminded of that episode in the classic *Star Trek* series on television, the one I cited in "The Sexual Theory of Everything," in which two aliens, the last of their kind, pursue one another across the galaxy in mortal combat. Symbolically, the actors portraying them are painted white on one side of their bodies and black on the other, compelling Mr. Spock to remark that they seem to be identical, but they are not exactly alike. There is that *obvious* distinction of reversed colors.

The smallest such differences, under the right historical circumstances, can spark the fire. If the other tribe is a different skin color or religion, it is inferior to us. If they have strange customs, dress differently, or eat exotic foods, perhaps they are not human, which means we are at liberty to kill them, take their land and any other wealth, and enslave their women and children. It would seem the destiny of human society to fall back into this primal state of barbarity in which, I must add, it survived for millions of years of evolution.

Civilization is still a relatively new and therefore fragile phenomenon. It has advanced the human condition some way on this planet so that we would dearly love to see it continue. I would like to think that, while we are still civilized, we might be able to observe and consider another person's heritage, his *breeding*, in an open and rational manner. Now the term itself has become code for white supremacy and the idiotic doctrine of racial purity, long discredited by science. Humankind did not evolve as separate races. Characteristic racial disparities in geographically isolated populations developed over time. Later explorers discovered exotic lands with strange people unrecognizable as brothers. Given our inherent propensities, incessant crossbreeding ensued. We are all mongrels.

Any person adopting a dog will consider the breed: Which one makes a good guard dog? What dog will I be able to trust with a new baby? Which may be expected to live long and be a loving, quiet companion? Know the breed, know the dog. Likewise, nothing prevents us from reckoning with the individual distinctiveness attributable to another person's heritage, taking it into account in the context of our own life, but let's show our own good breeding. Be fair and keep quiet about it.

MARRIAGE AND CHILDREN

- Bait and Switch -

I must preface this essay with the confession that I have no experience of marriage or children. I will nevertheless excuse my audacity with the credential of age, since one cannot live a goodly number of decades without gaining knowledge, casual or to some degree intimate, of many marriages and the families they fostered. There is a person's own family tree branching out, adding nephews, nieces, and cousins, and the families of numerous friends that one cannot but observe over the years. Standing back from the fray has made me a more objective observer. Being a good listener, I count many long-winded talkers among friends and acquaintances who like nothing better than to regale me with uncensored stories of their children and grandchildren and those of each relative, close or distant. As the subject is one that is considerably fraught, especially for the young, I feel compelled for their sake to contribute my reflections for the tuppence they may be worth.

I have touched upon this topic in other essays. "The Sexual Theory of Everything" says all that need be said: how life itself is defined by the primordial emergence of SROCs, how our hidden agenda in mating is to find the match that will produce the closest copy of ourselves. The essay "Choices" has a good deal to say about the perils of our most personal decisions: whom to marry and whether to have children. The essay "Breeding" argues for realistic considerations of ethnicity, religion, and social class in matchmaking. These are impersonal commentaries, while here I hope to relate with more specificity the familiar experiences.

The institution of marriage has a long history, the study of which fills countless volumes. It is freighted with this history and still expected, optimistically, to last for a person's life. In modern times, this momentous commitment is left to the young who are presupposed to enter it in their reproductive years. It would be hard to exaggerate the stress created by this expectation, as a perusal of the advice columns in the daily newspapers will show. A typical love triangle, for example, involves a young person physically attracted to someone who is exotic, exciting, and romantic but unreliable while being courted by another who is humdrum and boring yet the pillar of stability. Here a person must be tortured by the decision of whether to "settle," trying to imagine a lifetime of dull security and weigh it against the allure of the other—a life of thrilling romance that might well flame out with unbearable consequences.

Many people write for advice about weddings, which are now enormous extravaganzas. For the bride, it is the second and last time she will dress up, the first having been the high school senior prom. For her parents, it brings an expenditure second only to the home mortgage. Any uncertainty on the part of the wedding couple may easily be repressed for financial reasons alone. Brides and grooms have been left at the altar when one or the other becomes overwhelmed by the gravity of what that walk down the aisle signifies, while those too timid to disappoint family and friends—hundreds, perhaps, who have come to witness and celebrate—will face years confounded by doubt.

Still there are those who marry without reservation, certain of the mutuality of their love and thus the suitability of their choice. "True love," it was called by the old wives who believed it came along only once per person, akin to imprinting such as one encounters in waterfowl, a phenomenon that takes place when the hatchlings fix upon the first creature they encounter as their mother.

Conceivably such a thing might happen to pubescent humans, but to come upon the love of a lifetime is rare good fortune, and misfortune may intervene as in two disparate but famous cases. A young Abraham Lincoln did not wed his first true love, a girl who died at age twenty-two. He went on to wed Mary Todd, but in his spells of melancholia, did he brood on that first romance? Similarly, the Austrian composer Franz Joseph Haydn was in love with the young daughter of a wigmaker with whom he lodged. When the girl entered a convent, he made the fateful mistake of marrying her older sister. The two were unsuited, unhappy, and eventually took paramours. The haunting remembrance of a young love, the lingering and unremitting disappointment polluting, in comparison, all subsequent relationships—what do advice columns have to say about these miserable conditions?

One famous pearl of wisdom from Ann Landers to every unhappy wife in the late twentieth century was the question, "Are you better off with him or without him?" The genders were never reversed, because at that time, no woman could be better off without the support of the man's higher wage unless she were married to a compulsive gambler or abuser. The turn of the century required a new approach. Today's mavens seem bent upon doing their part to buttress the high rates of divorce. The virtue of a long marriage is lost upon them. They often advise with cavalier insouciance that the grass is greener on the other side of the fence; if at any time one's spouse begins to fall short of expectations, go forth and seek a better one! After some years of marriage, anyone may start to feel alienated for any number of reasons, deciding that his or her spouse is not the same person chosen long ago and thus concluding that there has been a "bait and switch."

In the last novel of Victorian author Thomas Hardy, *Jude the Obscure*, there is the perfect depiction of a typical matrimonial bait and switch. Poor Jude, who dreams of learning Latin in Christminster, the gleaming city he sees from a high hill in his small English town, is seduced by young Arabella, who conspires with her girlfriends to convince him that she is pregnant. They are rushed into marriage, and too late he discovers the ruse. Eventually, assured of a living as a stonemason, he leaves her behind and sets off to that far city, hoping to fulfill his life's dream. The tangled story of the ill-fated Jude gets worse from there, depicting the grave burden of social mores and religious strictures borne especially by the poor. An unsentimental honesty concerning marriage and the primal drives earned the author severe opprobrium from critics, which is seen as the reason Hardy never wrote another novel.

From the beginning, marriage is all about adapting to another person, and each one is often held back in some way by the other. Married women are historically susceptible to being denied any aspiration apart from mother and homemaker, but even in a broadminded couple, one spouse may refuse to move for the sake of the other's career advancement, or both can be kept from observing every holiday with their own relatives. No marriage can be maintained in a static condition as life changes, bringing new circumstances that challenge us to adapt. To stay married through it all demands resilience, spontaneity, and most of all, forbearance. Such character traits are the estimable product of a long marriage, as the maintenance of a stable relationship seasons our nature. The value lies in treating one another as valuable rather than as articles to be sampled and cast aside. We may show our merit by dogged persistence.

This is not to minimize the real difficulties that inevitably arise. No two people can be perfectly compatible, and too often their differences are obscured during courtship, when a young man may be extremely romantic toward the woman he loves only to drop the hand-holding once the knot is tied. If a man and woman are from different cultures, such disparities can cause considerable friction over time. In people watching, for example, I sometimes note a husband striding several yards in front of his wife, while she scurries behind at pains to keep up. These couples tend to be from characteristically machismo cultures. Will this habit spell trouble if his wife is of some other tribe, more accustomed to walking side by side, hand in hand? It may also be observed that the genders themselves, across all human societies, have their own dissimilar ways, contributing to the difficulty of married life.

Another pearl of wisdom oft repeated by Ann Landers summed up the major topics of discord for any married couple as "sex, money, and in-laws." If spouses can manage to get along in those three areas, there is hope.

In my essay "Communication," I cite the work of linguist Deborah Tannen, specifically her book *That's Not What I Meant*. Chapter seven, "Why Things Get Worse," addresses the frictions we are likely to see in long marriages. Here she explains: "Conventional wisdom and common sense tell us that the more time people spend together, the better they will understand each other" (Tannen 2011, 123). In other words, we commonly believe that two people can talk through their problems, when often, in the view of linguists, if differing styles of communicating have created a problem, more talking only makes things worse. We may assume what we say will be understood as we mean it, but the message might not get through when the listener responds more strongly not to the meaning of the words but to the metamessage.

The concept of the metamessage is remarkable in its irony and obscurity, because while extremely helpful, it is little known. As a wordsmith, I spent most of my life convinced that ideas are conveyed most effectively by choosing the right word; as true as this may be for written language, it is anything but when it comes to conversation. The metamessage is in the subtle cues—the tone of voice, facial expression, body language, and much more. Ironically, these are the focus of conversation, not the specific meanings of words, that can go in one ear and out the other. The metamessage is in the several paces maintained between striding husband and lagging wife; it might express his disregard for her safety or his confidence in her capability. The roses a husband may buy for Valentine's Day are a metamessage that may be received as an expression of caring or a useless waste of mutual resources. The overarching message for couples wanting to stay married is that they may afford one another the benefit of the doubt and safely refrain from thinking the worst, because maybe *that's not what he or she meant.*

In modern times, the single lifestyle has become more feasible and acceptable. Every person is unique, and individuals who cherish their independence and savor solitude should feel less social pressure to marry. Still there is in the young as they enter adulthood a lonely, yearning hunger that is common and natural and guides most people into the most intimate relationship. A good marriage will be one that, over time, is kept in a realistic perspective. When some incompatibility begins to seem insufferable, anyone who has reached the age of wisdom—sixty years according to the Chinese—should be able to compare it against a truly dire crisis: waiting captive in a medical office, for example, to learn whether the diagnosis is terminal. Bolstered by maturity, marriage is supportive through the inevitable travails. The ones that last into old age may be a salutary factor to the end—the final parting.

The matter of bearing children is equally as fraught as marriage if not more so. Before the era of modern birth control, there was little one could do to avoid the product of a normal sexual appetite. Notwithstanding, children were valued helpers on the farms and, before child labor laws, excellent factory workers. Even with the advent of effective tools for family planning, people still have wanted and, in spite of overpopulation, felt the primal drive to have children. Back in the mid to late twentieth century, when science warned of a "population bomb" threatening the world, ethologist John Calhoun's experiments with rodents demonstrated that the stress of overcrowding could in itself bring disastrous effects.[4] His "mouse universe" began with four pair of mice in a spacious enclosure. The colony rapidly became overcrowded with 2,200 mice. They stopped breeding, and before long, all were dead.

---

4. Wikipedia: John B. Calhoun. ("Death Squared: The Explosive Growth and Demise of a Mouse Population", 1973. Proc. R. Soc. Med. 66 (1 Pt 2): 80–88.)

Overcrowding aside, most young people are following the traditional pattern: marry, raise a family, retire, and ride off into the sunset of life. Could it be the unconscious influence of those SROCs from which we descend, the imperative to replace ourselves? To the young person, it may be the thing to do, or they may hope for the comfort and assurance of intimate family relationships, first with a spouse and then one's children and grandchildren. The business of heirs and heritage may loom large for some people.

However, I will venture to say—and I understate—that the true nature of child-rearing is not fully appreciated by those now willfully taking it on but comes as a shock to many young fathers and mothers. Realizing that in these times I risk rebuke or worse, I submit my view that women are the more ardently desirous of reproducing—a curious observation, given that they are the ones most burdened by the consequences. In comparison, many young men seem indifferent though persuadable. The sexual revolution threatened to diminish the role of fatherhood, which was once considered a social obligation, the inviolate responsibility to support one's progeny. While fathers are as important as ever to the health of society, the sentimental expectation now abroad that men will derive as much pleasure as their wives from the company of infants will likely be tested by this generation of fathers.

Excepting the extremely affluent, who can deposit the newborn with a live-in nanny in the nursery wing of the mansion, I suspect that untold numbers of young mothers, suddenly thrown into the onerous and unrelenting responsibility of a new baby, are daunted, to put it mildly. Often attributed to hormones, postpartum depression should to the contrary seem a natural result. Sleeplessness itself must be a factor for both parents. The only saving grace, the only thin reed upon which to cling, is that the child will grow up, be weaned, sleep through the night, walk and talk, and at some distant time, be a comfort in one's old age. Life is changed forever. Parenthood, for all its professed joys, is enormously burdensome on couples, emotionally and financially, and not to be entered into lightly.

Aggravating this burden are prevalent misconceptions of infants to which older generations were less susceptible. We used to hear the newborn referred to as "the little stranger," in acknowledgment that here was an individual whose nature was not yet known and to whom the parents must adapt. Now more commonly, the view of these new creatures is either of two errors: the baby as a blank slate, malleable to adult influence, or as the clone of a parent. In truth, the infant has a nature derived from a vast genetic heritage far deeper than two parents. The poor child must deal with this heritage, including those annoying adult influences, as he makes his way through life. He is a stranger, and when his parents discover unexpected inborn traits stubbornly resistant to correction or later recognize that their child will never be the brilliant scientist or gifted musician they were anticipating, there will be at least two decades during which they have ample opportunity to think they are the victims of "bait and switch."

Overly optimistic parents may fall prey to another fallacy: that they will be better parents than their own. While it is not a futile hope, it is unlikely. Well-known studies show that even people who have been physically abused as children grow up to be abusers themselves, repeating the parental example. The likelihood for all parents is that they will unconsciously fall into the familiar pattern they learned growing up. In several families of my acquaintance, I have observed this phenomenon with amazement: a mother or father who is adhering to conventions and practices handed down in the family while contending most vigorously that this is not the case. Perhaps in retrospect they will be objective enough to see it, but embroiled as they are in the day to day, they are blind—and equally as punctilious as Mother was or as penurious as Father.

There is a good deal of expertise available on the subject of child-rearing, and savvy young people today have ready access to it. A favorite of mine was *Supernanny*, a reality TV series released in the United Kingdom in 2004 and still available on the internet. It stars Joanne Frost as a traditional British nanny who each week takes on the case of a problem child, showing up at the home in a London taxi to instruct parents in the most effective child-rearing tools. These were unfailingly humane and rational, far from the nasty corporal punishment once visited upon those children referred to irately as "brats." I was impressed that these new methods were closely akin to the training of domestic animals—dogs and horses—that in my lifetime has become more humane and, as a result, more effective.

Years ago when I had occasion to take public transit, I sat next to an old Italian gentleman on a London double-decker. As is the wont of old men, perhaps especially Italians, he struck up a conversation, in the course of which he remarked that he could not understand why parents were always so worried about spoiling their children. He declared, with no small wisdom, that no matter what material gifts a parent may shower, children need not be adversely affected. So long as there is genuine love between parent and child, sincere gratitude will be the response.

Nevertheless, the outrageous knavery of those hard cases on *Supernanny* was more of a kind to inspire a severe thrashing than love, and the idea that such children could be tamed by patient, consistent, and implacable discipline, though demonstrated in most episodes, was dubitable. What was clear was how unprepared and unsuitable many adults are for parenthood. In many jurisdictions, public secondary schools require sex education, as though any animal needs to be instructed in this activity. Not that I am against it in terms of health and safety and in dispelling ignorant notions about the matter, but there should also be a course in marriage and child-rearing, perhaps as required training to receive a marriage license. I daresay people would have far fewer neuroses and society far less trouble with personality disorders.

As it is, a person comes of age and, with hormones raging, rushes headlong into what he or she believes will be a fulfilling lifetime, has fancies about what that life will be, and conceits about the nature of the ideal spouse, nearly all of which are delusions. Years go by, and the bloom is off the rose. Babies come along, and there are dreams of obedient children, loving companions in old age. Soon a wake-up call brings screaming infants followed by rebellious preteens, bad school grades, tattoos, and grotesque piercings.

The average person takes the bait of societal expectations, the assurance of fairytales, and real life turns out to be an intolerable "switch." By no means do I imply that this fate is universal, although half of the people who marry divorce and face even more adverse circumstances, personally and financially. Do those who stay married live happily ever after? We can only observe their commendable fortitude, resilience, humility, and good sense. Happiness is a bonus.

CHOICES

- As You Like It -

Choice is a good thing: it is good to be able to choose how you will make a living, where you will live, and whom you will marry. Likewise we appreciate having options when we go to the multi-acre big box market or scroll through millions of items in millions of categories on a website. In this respect, thanks to the spread of consumerism across the globe, a panoply of choice available to a large swath of the human population now exists. Not only do we have more options, the number of those options for any given product one might name grows exponentially. It would seem choice is metastatic in modern life, yet I venture to say there is a limit, that being the point when every living person will be paralyzed with indecision. The important decisions in life have always had some inherent difficulty, and we are not helped when navigating our everyday lives becomes an obstacle course of decision making. It was not always thus.

In Britain after World War II, when I was coming along, there were shortages of consumer goods well into another decade. The only choice for many people was to "make do and mend," as the saying went. By contrast, America, which had not suffered the devastation of bombing on its shores, was becoming a great capitalist engine driven by consumer demand.

Even in the States, however, there were not many choices, and people seemed happy, glad to have options and never imagining there should be more. Ice cream came in vanilla, chocolate, and strawberry. No one ate yogurt. Breakfast cereal was Kellogg's Corn Flakes or Wheaties. The family car was a Ford, Chrysler, or Chevrolet. These were available in colors by then unlike the Model T, which Henry Ford was famously quoted as saying could be had in any color "as long as it's black." When television was born in the 1950s, programs were broadcast by NBC, ABC, or CBS. We British, meanwhile, made do with the BBC, referred to fondly as "Auntie" for its straitlaced standards.

In the late-twentieth century, a veritable blossoming in every product category began to happen. A good example is Ford Motors, not long content with the black Model T. Along came Lincoln and then Mercury. By the 1960s, the latter branch was proliferating egregiously: there was the Mercury Monterey, Montclair, Montego, Marquis, Monarch, and on and on ad nauseam. In time, American auto companies faced serious competition from the Asians, who had their own proliferation of brands and models. Mercury was defunct by 2011, but never fear, Toyota had plenty of choices: Camry, Corolla, Highlander, Forerunner, Solara, Lexus, and others that escape my memory.

Peruse any aisle of a supermarket today, and the proliferation of varieties on the shelves is astonishing in its excess. Whatever the product, there are multiple competing brands, each of which must offer every conceivable configuration of the thing. I am told by one amiable employee who stocks the dairy cases at my local supermarket that there are some five hundred different kinds of yogurt alone. One may choose the Greek style or regular, nonfat, low fat, and lactose free, each variety in myriad flavors or plain. Factor in the many brands that must supply the full extent of these offerings, the number explodes, and yogurt fills the store.

The phenomenon is a huge problem that I call "proliferitis," and I believe that globalization must be the root cause. No longer dependent on domestic production, we expect the whole world to satisfy our demands to the most minute specification. For retailers, there is the headache of trying to carry the rapidly expanding number of products in a finite space, but the consumer also finds himself disadvantaged, especially if he is a creature of habit. If the sale of his favorite flavor, brand, or color of something drops off, the item will be sidelined to a lower shelf, then inevitably discontinued to make room for the latest fad. A favorite of mine years ago was a nondairy frozen dessert called Toffutti, concocted of tofu to replace ice cream for those like myself who are allergic. It was found at the bottom of the freezer cabinet, but the manager seemed to know his customers to the extent that if even one of them was partial to Toffutti Love Drops, which had bits of chocolate and graham cracker, he kept it stocked. It was a favorite of mine, but when the store changed managers, it disappeared.

Surely, you protest, anything can now be found on the internet from the comfort of home on your handheld device, even lactose-free, nonfat, Greek-style, strawberry cheesecake-flavored yogurt—or I daresay Toffutti Love Drops. Order it, charge it, and voila—delivered to your door by drone! In my experience, however, websites are as labyrinthine as the most enormous of the big box stores. By the time one has filtered through numerous criteria and scrolled page after page looking for one specific thing only to conclude that it is not there, one may as well have hopped in the car, driven to a store, and settled for whatever was to be had. The internet is time consuming, its alleged efficiency a mirage.

How is it, I am caused to wonder, that we have come to expect every product we consume or use to be made exactly to our individual preference? There is something infantile about it, which I am not alone in observing. The infantilization of the consumer is a recognized tool in the marketing arsenal. Just stand on line at Starbucks waiting impatiently for a tall coffee while the customer five ahead in queue dithers about a grande decaf soy mocha frappuccino light. Get caught behind the person at the deli ordering a sandwich who needs to see the corned beef, to know what types of bread he may have, what kind of cheese, what brand of mustard or horseradish, and how fresh the pickles. There comes a threshold, I fear, at which society grinds to a halt.

The matter of choice goes beyond consumerism. It has a political aspect as well. In communist countries, the government ownership of the means of production impedes the economy, inhibiting choice. The Soviet Union was notoriously grim and the butt of jolly mockery for its dull monotony. A television commercial for Wendy's from the 1980s spoofed a Russian fashion show with but one rotund model dressed like a charwoman. In the most robust Russian accent, the announcer cries, "Is next, svimvear!" and out comes the charwoman carrying a beach ball. "Is next, evening vear!" and here she comes with a flashlight. The voiceover says, "Having no choice is no fun," going on to tout the Wendy's hamburger prepared to a customer's preference. The free world stands in sharp contrast not only for being more fashionable or allowing a choice of hamburger toppings, but, more importantly, for the freedom of citizens to elect their leaders. The unfortunate fact that this latter freedom is hampered lately in the liberal democracies raises a little-noticed irony in the aforementioned burgeoning of choice.

Oddly, the seeming infinity of choice breeds conformity. From yogurt flavors to yoga pants, we tend to choose the same thing, creating fads, which reduces options by eliminating whatever the so-called "hive mind" of pop culture ignores. Our nature as a social species inhibits our freedom to choose. Following the herd in order to belong, we wear the same clothes, listen to the same music, and eat at the same fast-food outlets. Thus does conformity defy superfluous choice. Translated to a democratic political process, the phenomenon inevitably forces candidates to conform to the latest polls. In a vicious cycle, the one highest in the polls gets more attention at the expense of all the others, thereby rising still higher and getting *more* attention. A true leader cannot be customized like a deli sandwich or a cup of coffee, and too often, individuals with the most leadership ability are left out, to our universal misfortune.

Choice is a good thing until it is too much choice, overwhelming our ability to choose. With too many decisions, how do we decide? The answer would appear to be more scientific than philosophical, bearing as it does on studies of the brain and neurochemistry. Motivations in human behavior arise and respond to electrochemical tides in the brain. Even the conscious choices we make are coerced by uncontrolled forces. In the choice of a mate, for example, it has been demonstrated through experiment that people are attracted to members of the opposite sex who have the physical features associated with fertility. Against our conscious will, we may choose the attractive person and reject one who is more compatible because of a lack of "chemistry." There is a subconscious process to choice whether we are deciding on a mate or even what to eat. We choose foods high in fat, sugar, or salt, for example, because they are addictive, and addiction is an unconscious, irresistible appetite. When this property was revealed in studies, the food processing industry learned to manipulate these ingredients, contributing to obesity and the ill health of the populace.

Damasio's book, mentioned in two previous essays, shows how emotion, even in its weaker manifestation as attitude, colors all our actions. He begins with the case of Phineas P. Gage, a railroad foreman and an expert with explosives who, in the mid-nineteenth century, survived a horrendous accident that blew an iron rod through the frontal lobe of his brain. (The skull of Phineas Gage is on display at Harvard Medical School.) He recovered miraculously and seemed to return to normal, but as time went by, it was clear that his personality was altered, and he had lost all executive function. He could not complete a day's work because he could not choose what was important and would perseverate over the trivial. The damage to his brain had involved an area responsible for emotion, without which he was unable to prioritize. Damasio demonstrates that emotion is involved to some degree in even the smallest daily decisions.

If we look closely at the phenomenon of choice, we see that people would be just as satisfied with less of it. They were so in generations past, and they are now when they neglect to participate in all but a fraction of the choices offered. Imagine how long it would take to sample all five hundred permutations of yogurt brands, flavors, textures, and other attributes. Of course, the proliferation of products is an economic good—more jobs, more sales, and happier customers. As in the Wendy's ad, to have no choice is no fun, but then, what is too much choice?

I would submit that the threshold lies at some point where the constant sorting of the stuff of life becomes all-consuming. We have reached that point already when, mysteriously, we have slow growth despite full employment. The cause is inefficiency. Who has time to produce anything when every basic task of life involves searching a haystack for a needle? Click on "Font," and see how many you must scroll past every time you want "Times." Moreover, few people are adept at making decisions, becoming flummoxed by too many choices.

Consider the odd fate of television networks, originally broadcasting over the air to antennas connected to the sets in our homes—for free. There were but a few networks making a living through commercials until cable television was born. The idea that consumers would pay for television when they might have it free of charge was laughable except for two inducements: cable would have no commercials and would offer innumerable channels. As it gained in popularity, cable companies could not resist selling commercial time, and still, abiding equally as many ads as they would see on the old networks, subscribers stuck with cable. The cable companies began to compete on the basis of that second inducement: they could offer *hundreds* more channels than the competition! Too much choice. Consumers began to notice that they were paying for hundreds of channels in which they had no interest. It was the death of television. Today, in place of watching television, people *stream* entertainment on computers, which have hybridized with the television.

The more consequential decisions are those we face are in our personal lives where, for example, we encounter the highly charged political use of the word "choice" as buzzword. The legalization of abortion, along with the development of more reliable means of birth control, introduced the previously unimaginable ability—aside from total celibacy—to choose whether to have children. Most people have continued to want children and have benefited in being able to plan their families, but the decision is not easy for everyone and should be left to those bearing its enormous consequences. Babies can overtax the emotions of an immature or unbalanced young person unprepared for parenthood who has succumbed to hormones or conformed to tribal pressure. How many sociopathic—or at least neurotic—individuals grow to troubled adulthood as a result is impossible to measure, but psychiatrists are kept busy.

At the opposite end of life lie other controversial choices. Should the terminally ill be allowed the means for a peaceful, dignified death, and should their doctors be able to supply it? These questions were settled by the ancient Greeks who gave us the word euthanasia, which I explore in another essay. It is most curious that a civilization descended from those ancients should have moved so far from their obvious wisdom. In modern times, when we live long enough to fall victim to degenerative disease and cancers, the latter ever ready to overtake the immune system weakened by age, death comes only after protracted torture while mercy is reserved for our animals.

A person who is dying should be able to choose a more merciful means than nature exacts, but we have a peculiar and stubborn bias to "choose life," as it says on the anti-abortion bumper sticker. There is a common attitude that life is natural and natural is good, but somehow death is not natural. Death is as natural as life and necessary to maintain balance in the ecosphere, yet we see nothing wrong morally or philosophically with taking extreme measures to prevent death, while to interfere with conception and birth is against God. The inference is that we have an unnatural God.

Our unreason on the subject is a reflection of the definition of life, the subject of the first essay in this collection. We are absurdly unreasoning in our blinkered one-sidedness concerning birth and death, being the most advanced kindred in that primordial lineage of SROCs. Unfortunately, that unreason could lead to our extinction when our numbers overwhelm planetary resources. We might succeed in extinguishing every living thing but the cockroach.

Choices lie on a wide spectrum from the trivial to the significant, even grave ones. As we make our decisions among options, we spin the roulette wheel in the casino of life—for whatever stakes at whatever odds. Is this not the uncertainty that makes a decision unnerving, even intimidating? If you choose a new flavor of yogurt that turns out not to be to your taste, you can feed it to the dog or throw it away, but who has not had the experience of opting for a menu item only to reconsider when it arrives, realizing the petite fillet would have been preferable to the prime rib? Some individuals have such an anxiety when it comes to choosing that the process leaves them fretting interminably, spending all afternoon, we might imagine, in the dairy aisle.

Concerning a more important of life's decisions, the high rate of divorce is a statistic that reflects the number of people who have second thoughts when it comes to marriage. While other social species rely on combat among eligible males to determine reproductive rights, humans do not seem to have found a reliable way to choose a mate. In cultures with a long tradition of arranged marriage, the firm belief is that the elders have the experience and wisdom to match their children with compatible partners. Nonetheless, those elders may seek some advantageous alliance with another tribe, irrespective of a happy marriage, which is then unlikely. Unhappiness becomes the norm. Western societies have for some centuries held that love is the answer, that two young people falling in love could be counted on to form a stable family, but youngsters in their fertile years are easily misled by hormones and caught up in multiple passions—not conducive to stability.

Those parts of Europe where the Roman Empire held sway—from Spain and France to the British Isles—were bequeathed the odd legacy of chivalry, the noble code of the cavalry soldier, the armored knight on horseback. The actual history of chivalry as an institution is lost in the fog of the medieval Dark Age, yet as celebrated in literature, the chivalrous ideal of championing the weak—women in particular—would seem unique to Western civilization. Was it the lingering influence of that closet Buddhist, Jesus? Where else in the world do we find a sport equivalent to the jousting tournaments with knights, in honor of their ladies, tilting lances at each other from horseback? Still, even romance with the winning knight has not proven the sure path to marital bliss. Many a poor soul, inclined toward physical attraction, has chosen the sexy but fickle suitor. Hence the divorce rate.

It is a sad prospect as we move through life to find ourselves persuaded that long ago we made the wrong choice of mate, that now we are yoked by time, assets, and progeny to someone we no longer recognize. This unhappy conclusion is misguided and shows the common tendency to rewrite our personal history. In retrospect, we easily forget how we felt in the throes of youthful passion unless we try harder to remember. Furthermore, we are not the same in different life stages. We change dramatically from courting, mating, and nesting in the prime of life to the empty nest and old age. To stay in a marriage requires a willingness and flexibility to adapt to one another through these changes and not expect to maintain the fervor of youth.

Today we turn to the internet as the answer to all things. Advice columns are passé. Ann Landers is gone to her well-deserved reward. We have Match.com and other websites. With enough psychological sophistication and a carefully nuanced questionnaire, a website may conceivably bring together two strangers—to find themselves amazingly compatible. The idea seems far more palatable and efficient than the long, awkward process of dating random acquaintances, especially given the rules of recent generations that require immediate exclusivity. Courting in sequence, one individual at a time, could easily consume the entire span of one's procreative years. The ticking of that biological clock adds urgency to this choice, but as for determining compatibility, we should remain skeptical of these dating sites, considering the track record of colleges in matching roommates. Two students can seem on the surface to be ideally suited to share a dorm room, but put them together, and their wholly dissimilar temperaments may come out.

The major decisions of our lives involve serious choices, often among limited options or even between evils: whom to wed, whether to have children, "to be or not to be." Shakespeare captured the weightiness of the matter perfectly in Hamlet's soliloquy: "Whether 'tis nobler in the mind to suffer the slings and arrows of outrageous fortune, or to take arms against a sea of troubles and by opposing end them." Such are the choices life forces on us, while in our daily lives we are bombarded by trivial ones, constantly changing and increasing. For example, the word processing application Word opens on Home where we see in the toolbar tabs Font, Paragraph, Styles, Insert, and Themes, under each of which are approximately a dozen buttons that one may choose to click. In addition to Home, at the same level there appear Layout, Document Elements, Tables, Charts, Smart Art, and Review, and under each of these, dozens more buttons to select. Do the math—I get more than four hundred decisions to make, none of which has ever provided the result I am looking for. Add to this all the other types of office software, not to mention programs customized for the professions, and you see why your poor doctor spends the five minutes he has allotted to your visit fiddling with his laptop. Life is complicated enough, fraught with uncertainty and confounded by distraction. By worsening these factors, we are losing the meaning of things in a chaos of inexplicable gibberish.

An essay on choice must perforce discuss perhaps the most important one for a writer: word choice. In any genre, the selection of the right word may strike the spark of success for a piece, and writers go to great lengths looking for that word, poring over a heavy thesaurus or, these days, searching online dictionaries. With age, the task is increasingly problematic, as instant recall grows less and less instant. I call it "intention tremor of the brain." As long as one tries to recall a word or name, it does not come; stop trying to think of it, and there it is. Meaning, however, frequently requires special care to use the one proper word. A story is credible, for example, if it offers reasonable grounds to be believed. If it is not only worthy of belief but also "sufficiently good to bring esteem or praise," per *Merriam-Webster's Collegiate Dictionary*, it is creditable.

Surely, words are not subject to the same exponential proliferation we have noted. We choose them from our language, which we might expect to have some stability during our lifetime. Alas, even our words have accreted enormously. The pages of the aforementioned dictionary must now be as thin as tissue paper to hold all the words we might need to choose from.

There is my point. The world is always changing; change is the only constant. Once, generations could pass before change was noticeable. Today, not a single one has gone by before the old is obsolete. From the time Alexander Graham Bell was awarded a patent for the telephone in 1876, it took three generations or more before his invention came into widespread use. In contrast, no one now living is recognizable by society without a smartphone, a technology that has existed for one generation. This device gives us choices for communicating via text, voice, social media, email, or video. A child can do it without his parents knowing any better—or even how to reach him.

The ever-faster proliferation of new varieties, new options—those five hundred kinds of yogurt in the dairy aisle—is destabilizing when it takes place in less than a lifetime. The old are isolated, unable to share the relative wisdom of their experience, while the young are more burdened than they can realize, having no basis for comparison. The latter are born into high tech; they are facile with it before preschool, but it follows that they also have no knowledge of low tech: how easy it is to look at your wrist watch for the time or whip out your daybook to scribble a note without having to deal with the screen and the keypad of your mini-computer, still known as a "phone." Taking the breakneck pace as normal—all they have known—their life span is shortened. A chronic, protracted state of stress or alertness has been reliably associated with damage to the immune system and thus a shorter life.

Perhaps change is good after all; you can have everything you want—your burger, your yogurt, your car, your next love affair—just *as you like it!* You will never have to prove yourself against Charles the Wrestler as did Orlando, courting the hand of the lovely Rosalind in Shakespeare's romantic comedy *As You Like It*. George Bernard Shaw disparaged this play as not of the playwright's best, suggesting that it may have been written as a crowd pleaser, and he may have been right about the rom-com. When Rosalind, fleeing her angry uncle, disguises herself as Ganymede, the fetching shepherd boy of Greek myth, the humorous gender ambiguity would have pleased Shakespeare's audience, especially those who took the inference that *As You Like It* has something to do with that most gorgeous of all mortal males, Jove's own page!

MODERNISM

- *But Is It Art?* -

The reader will surmise from my subtitle that I am not a fan of modern art. I regard a painting such as *The Snail* by Matisse, where colored squares of paper were glued to canvas by his assistant in 1953, as an abundance of Tartuffery hardly concealing a dearth of cleverness. As for the grandfather of modern art, Picasso, I will not conceal my distaste for the notorious misogynist. After his 1907 painting *Les Demoiselles d'Avignon* was met with repulsion and shock, even from Matisse, a critic wrote, "It was the ugliness of the faces that froze with horror the half-converted."[5] I remain among those frozen with horror in the image of *The Scream* by another modern artist, Norwegian Edvard Munch. This is not a treatise on modernism but rather a personal look at its lingering effects on our lives and culture.

According to Merriam-Webster, one definition of modernism is "a self-conscious break with the past and a search for new forms of expression." It refers commonly to a movement in Western culture that arose in the late-nineteenth century in response to the industrial revolution and the rapid growth of cities, which brought dramatic social change. The impact of World War I, the revolt against traditional bourgeois values, and the rejection of realism gave birth to the avant-garde: abstract art, atonal music, and the stream-of-consciousness fictional style. At first meeting with skep-

---

5. Andre Salmon "Pablo Picasso's Les Demoiselles d'Avignon 1907." Culture Shock. PBS.

ticism to the point of hostility, this "vanguard" of creative rebels gradually became so firmly entrenched in the twentieth century that modernism continues to dictate what is established as acceptable in the twenty-first, well past an era when it might still have been considered "modern." Might it now be time to reconsider this rigid, superannuated creed? I am willing.

Recognizing that science progresses steadily, modernists embraced the assumption that the arts should also advance, yet art is a form of language, the attempt to communicate with others verbally, musically, or visually. People can accept evolutionary changes in their language and continue to understand one another, and in the Western world, such an evolution of the arts in past centuries enhanced the ability to communicate. The revolutions of the twentieth century destroyed that communication. Modern artists, in all media, more often have taken pride in being misunderstood by the masses.

THE VISUAL ARTS

For centuries, even millennia if you include the prehistoric cave drawings of France, painting was about the depiction in two dimensions of three-dimensional visual reality, but the modern artist abandoned this realism. The invention of photography in the late nineteenth century was the major influence, driving artists to abstraction, literally and perhaps figuratively. The first departure from tradition was Impressionism; visual reality was still depicted but in such a way as to convey the artist's impression of it. What continues to come across, even more so than in a realistic style, is the artistic yearning to capture, along with the image, the moods or emotions it evokes. The canvasses of Cezanne, Monet, Renoir, Gauguin, and others show that painting was still superior in this respect to the upstart invention of photography. The gifted painters of any era realize intuitively that in their interpretation of what is seen, they add their inner vision to the optical one. For those misguided painters who saw as their main or only function the accurate rendering of landscapes or portraits, now replaced by the camera, the answer was abstract modern art.

As soon as abstract art had seeped into the mainstream of culture, it begged the question of what art really is, and it had undermined all the criteria by which painting had previously been judged. Who could say that an abstract work had been drawn or composed well when we had forsworn the gold standard of sight? If it need not be true to an objective reality upon which all viewers could agree, its value was free to fluctuate upon the vagaries of the subjective. There have been attempts to invent new objective criteria—the use of color or line, optical effects, expressionistic, or even sociopolitical depth—but these have been easily shot down by artists obstinately opposed to being judged at all. We might concur that the new role of artist as poet or social conscience is equal or superior to that of illustrator or scene and portrait painter, but we must accept as a consequence that any work of art may now be worthless or priceless.

By the late twentieth century, the world of fine art had turned away from painting completely, abstract or otherwise. Any individual could express himself in any new form conceivable, and it would be called "art." This untethering of the concept gave the world such appalling examples as street art, performance art, and the latest—installation art. The latter appears to be the province of the mentally deranged, as for example the person who coated the walls and ceiling of a closet with beeswax, illuminating it with a bare lightbulb dangling above the perplexed spectator. More Tartuffery. Less disturbing and more typical are installations that tend to be large, intricate, mind-numbing constructions, impressive chiefly in their extravagant and garish complexity: vast museum halls filled with tall forms built of cardboard tubes or the "infinity mirror room" with sixty-plus glowing pumpkin sculptures, the work of Japanese artist Yayoi Kusama. These would seem to be made by those afflicted with severe obsessive-compulsive disorder.

Far from the high chieftains of fine art, a vast arena of painting still goes on, appreciated and purchased by the common people with their own personal tastes as criteria. Some of this work is good, and some such artists can make a living from it. Will it be preserved without society as a whole having bestowed its attention? The fate of such art, worthy as it might be, seems sealed in oblivion.

MODERN MUSIC

If memory serves, it was at a prestigious university where I attended a piano recital at which the performer played no music. He did sit at the piano, but over the sound system, the audience heard only the sizzle of an egg frying. I was among the majority of the disgusted patrons who arose and left. This chicanery was reminiscent of extremist John Cage, whose 4'33" has performers stand onstage for four minutes and thirty-three seconds—not a musical piece at all, just brief Zen practice. More typical, at least in the arena of so-called serious music, has been atonal composition.

Like the art of painting, the language of Western music evolved over hundreds of years, flowering from the seventeenth century on. An elaborate tonal syntax resulted, based upon the octave scale and the harmonic interrelationships arising from it. This musical scale, unique in the world, was invented in ancient Greece through the effort to discover the "music of the spheres" and was derived from the acoustical properties of vibrating media. We call it the Pythagorean scale after its inventor, the ancient Greek mathematician. The eight tones of our scale, in a natural hierarchy determined by the harmonic series, have opened for composers an infinity of creative potential that is not possible using more primitive scales with fewer tones.

The repertoire of musical masterpieces using this scale is accepted and loved by people around the world. An excellent and thorough book on the subject is *Music, the Brain, and Ecstasy* by Robert Jourdain. Explaining the science, math, and history of it most eloquently, the author also suggests that the scale may have a certain resonance with the human brain, being founded in a natural phenomenon. In simple terms, tone is created by vibration that results in sound waves of a given frequency, or wavelength, determining the pitch. Divide the vibrating medium in half—say a string or hollow tube of air—and the frequency doubles. This tone is an octave above the original, and our ears hear it as the same sound, only higher. By continuing to divide the medium, we derive the sequential tones of the harmonic series and end up with our octave scale. Sound frequency is mathematically infinite; think of the slide of a trombone or a sighing gypsy violin. Our eight-note scale plus five chromatic notes, for a total of twelve semitones in the octave, have proven the ideal number our brains may be expected to discern.

This common musical language united Western culture from Russia to America, and our ears were and still are as attune to its vocabulary as to a mother tongue. In a tonal composition, the hierarchy of the scale notes produces a tonal center, recognized as such by even the untutored ear. This phenomenon explains why musical masterpieces of the past are glorious beyond doubt: the intricate musical tapestries of Bach, the architecture of a Beethoven symphony, the soaring harmonies of Rachmaninoff, the lyrical, haunting melodies of Schubert, the rhythmic power of Liszt. Because of such genius, we speak of music as the language of emotion. Upon the dawn of the twentieth century, the urge toward liberation from the fetters of convention took hold, overthrowing the regime of the scale and robbing this language of human significance. The resulting "atonal" music invented by Schoenberg, Berg, Webern, and others uses the same twelve tones in a deliberately democratic way, forsaking the tonal center of gravity as though the chromatic notes had been crying out for justice and equality. The listener is left adrift in random sound. Atonal music arouses no emotion, speaks to no one, and appeals to no one, yet the music establishment does not allow a living composer to use that great legacy of ancient Greece, the Pythagorean scale. A commercial failure, modern music typically gets an obligatory nod before orchestras return to their bread and butter: the pre-twentieth-century repertoire.

Tonality persisted in other spheres such as popular song and musicals on stage and screen. Thanks to these, there is still a place for songs we all can sing. Popular music, deprived of the contribution of gifted and trained songwriters, devolved into three-note chants and then, abandoning tone completely, so-called rap music.

Revolution in the creative arts, especially music, was rooted in a misconception of the artist as free spirit and free agent. The notion that the individual artist could express in his own way the heights and the depths of human experience, insight, and intuition was new in the nineteenth century. Prior to that, he was beholden to the church or the aristocracy, social bastions providing a cultural climate that gave him permission, as heir to a common language, to communicate universal meaning in that language. Beethoven might be considered the first free agent, spurning servitude and succeeding where Mozart had failed to earn his livelihood through performing and publishing his music. Franz Liszt comes to mind as the first superstar, paving the way for the modern artist. An excellent biography of this towering figure, written in 1974 by Eleanor Spencer Stone, is subtitled *The Artist as Romantic Hero*.

LITERATURE

The realm of literature by no means avoided the upheaval of the avant-garde. The modern way became "stream of consciousness," being a narrative style purporting to capture the train of thought in the mind of the protagonist. *Ulysses*, written in 1922 by James Joyce, is the most famous example, but an obscure, extreme specimen of the style, written in 1949 in the Irish language, has in the English translation the title *The Dirty Dust*. It records the whisperings in an Irish graveyard among those buried there. In a postmortem stream of consciousness, the dead continue to gossip, quarrel, and question the newly buried about the world aboveground, their families, and their descendants. From these tidbits of macabre conversation, the reader is at pains to piece together their stories.

More recently, I note a trend similar to those mind-numbing constructions of installation art. I was given a copy of the prize-winning novel *The Luminaries*, over eight hundred pages, set in New Zealand at the time of their gold rush but involving also the signs of the zodiac. Is it a murder mystery, a ghost story, or a treasure hunt? The alleged genius of its twenty-eight-year-old author escaped me, and I gave up on it. The writing was so excruciatingly meticulous that it seemed she had been hired by a motion picture company to transcribe a recording of the director's verbal instructions. I never discovered what the constellations had to do with it, but I observed another sign that obsessive-compulsive disorder may take one to the top of the creative arts these days.

In contrast to this painstaking madness, we should observe the laziness that characterizes modern poetry. Rhyme and rhythm are forsaken, left to rappers, and free verse is the exclusive new form. Free verse is easy, while to write a poem in a certain meter and make it rhyme is not, and the justification has been that a rhyming verse is only doggerel, that nothing meaningful can be expressed the old-fashioned way. This assumption is easily disputed with the poems of such greats as Robert Frost or Edna St. Vincent Millay, my personal favorites. The ingenious pattern of Frost's "Stopping by Woods on a Snowy Evening," "The Road Not Taken," or "My November Guest," the wisdom conveyed in "Renascence," written by a nineteen-year-old Millay, demonstrate a mastery reliant on serious effort. That is poetry. Rappers come close albeit with feminine rhymes.

The fate of modern literature was interrupted with the advent of the internet, which brought the e-book and print on demand, sending publishing houses scrambling for survival in the unwonted competition. Editors at a handful of these old-line businesses had been the customary arbiters, filtering what options the reading public would see. With modern technology, the man on the street can publish his own manuscript. Swamped with such competition, the large companies now publish only what they solicit from authors whose names are recognized and therefore proven best sellers. No more avant-garde experiments foisted on a long-suffering reading public!

THE FUTURE OF FINE ARTS

Today, the fine arts have been marginalized, because at the highest levels they have been removed from the community, from people. The heirs of Wagner and Liszt, Monet and Cezanne, Dickens and Hardy have squandered a wealthy estate, unable to renew its capital, having turned their backs on its source: the interest and love of their fellow man. The Romantic artist seized his freedom from traditional institutions, and the modern artist forsook that freedom for the ivory tower—and an audience of the initiated few individuals who profess to see the emperor's new clothes. This elite group of cognoscenti continues to believe that the purest and truest artistic expression, the most philosophically meaningful, is achieved only when the artist is beholden to no one nor constrained by considerations of style or aesthetics. The utilitarian functions to create a thing of beauty for others to admire, to compose music for worshipers to sing in church, are disparaged.

It may be true that the truly creative individual with his superior vision must tread a lonely path accompanied only by the rara avis who shares that vision, but must we call his work art? Artistic expression should be an act of communication; therefore, whatever lonely path one might follow in pursuit of whatever solitary revelation will not lead to the creation of art unless or until one is able to share that vision with other people. When we say that a masterpiece has stood the test of time, we mean that its creator has captured a vision so clear that it is recognized by all over generations. Bach can still sell cars; Schoenberg never could nor ever will.

The modern arts are too facile in rejecting the hard work of communication on the arrogant assumption that the masses of people cannot understand greatness anyway. On the contrary, the great masses of people can and do understand true greatness. They always have been and will continue to be the final arbiters of what belongs in that category. If in centuries to come the art works of our time fall into oblivion, it will be their judgment. If perchance the unpublished novel, the dusty canvas, or the moth-eaten manuscripts of our unsung contemporaries are rescued from that oblivion by succeeding generations, that too would be the peoples' verdict. Ultimately, art is democratic.

What is the likelihood of that last scenario of a great writer, painter, or composer living, working, and dying in obscurity in the twenty-first century? In society today, there is no leavening to give rise to such activity. The milieu in which our children grow gives the distinct message that artistic expression is frivolous, while if a child can send a ball consistently through a hoop, balance on a beam, and do somersaults in the air, he or she stands to win the lavish admiration and extravagant adulation of the adult world. We should not be surprised that a young person would rather play basketball than take piano lessons when his options at the keyboard are unappealing *modern* pieces or music written centuries ago. When creative genius is funneled universally into computer science, we are in a sad, ugly time. I suspect that even Mozart, had he been raised in such an atmosphere, would have been discouraged. For the true creative artist, there must be some realistic hope that someone will see or hear and care about his work.

Is modernism the death of art, the extinction at the end of a long and brilliant evolution? Do we leave only relics of past glory and no living tradition within which new people can continue to create anew?

If the arts are to resume their historic course, this will come from converging sources. Should the elite fine arts gradually if grudgingly come back to the common artistic languages, the vogue of the incomprehensible may fade. Realism may again find a niche and tonal music gain acceptance. When the artistic establishment moves in this direction, the main avenue for the creative artist at last opens again.

At the same time, those arenas that have all along been producing what some might call schlock—the sofa art, pop music, and Broadway shows—will in some cases mature. An occasional artist may make enough money to allow him to do more serious work and command wider attention in the art world. It is interesting that in musical theater, darker, more serious themes have been taken up: *Phantom of the Opera*, with its rhapsodic melodies, and *Les Miserables*, whose composer ironically has the surname Schoenberg.

What would finally allow this development would be a transformation in aesthetics: in other words, a change in our definition of beauty. As long as we agreed on that definition, all was well for the arts. A graphic work had to be drawn well to be beautiful; a musical composition had to adhere to acceptable melodic intervals and harmonic progressions. Modern artists, in breaking these molds, showed us that beauty can be otherwise, can have eccentric lines and unexpected sounds, but they went too far. While it is true that the common perception of beauty is subjective and variable, we need not have abandoned artistic standards to that subjectivity. Beauty may no longer be defined as before, but it is not beyond definition. Again, artists have shrunk from the task, preferring the ease of anarchy.

Modernism stripped the arts of beauty, but here is where the subject touches upon philosophy, since the modern style, by redefining art, extirpated the definition of beauty. The arts, in this modern philosophy, must express truth, and truth, goes the audacious assertion, is not beautiful but ugly. If the objective is to represent truth, we are compelled to capture the quintessential ugliness of modern life—uglier by far, claims the modern artist, than at any prior time including prehistory. A clear-eyed perspective of history tells us that modern civilization is not exceptional in this respect. Consider the nineteenth century: the wars, diseases, and crowding in filthy cities. Was Monet oblivious to pollution when in 1872 he painted *Impression, Soleil Levant,* a watery rendering of sunrise through haze and smoke, over ships and smokestacks? Did he recoil at the filthy air and throw his paints into the channel? Was Beethoven driven by ill health and the hideous fate of his deafness to invent atonal music? Hardly that. Three years before he died, his ninth and last symphony was performed, ending with the chorus singing the immortal "Ode to Joy" to the words of poet Friedrich Schiller, which demolished the philosophical defense of modernism: "Alle menschen werden brüder wo dein sanfter flugel weilt" ("All people become brothers where your gentle wing abides"). Maynard Solomon, in his 1977 biography of Beethoven, observed, "If we lose the dream of the Ninth Symphony there remains no counterpoise against the engulfing terrors of civilization" (Solomon 1977, 315). Beethoven himself wrote, "Only art and science give us intimations and hopes of a higher life" (Solomon 1977, 316).

Perhaps beauty is beyond words, yet while it is the artist who reveals beauty, he needs the rest of us to tell him whether he has succeeded. How do *we* know? What is our guiding aesthetic? How are single works selected through centuries to be regarded as masterpieces? In the oeuvre of Beethoven, it is not compliance with standards of form and rules of harmony that make them special; nor do they overwhelm us with innovation. Beethoven uses common musical language to guide the listener, comforting him with familiarity, surprising him on occasion but always leading him to share the vision, which is paramount.

Reflect upon any Impressionist painting, a supremely evocative style: for example, Monet's *Jardin a Sainte-Adresse,* painted in 1867 and now in the Metropolitan Museum of Art. Without being meticulously realistic, the foreground of the summer flower garden draws us in: a clear day, wind whipping the flags, boats in the distance on the cobalt waters of the English Channel. Two couples in Victorian dress—the women with parasols, one man in a top hat, the other in a straw fedora—create a sense of the season. The air, the light, the sounds and smells create an *impression* of summer that stirs the memory along with its attendant emotion.

As for literature, one need read only the first page of *A Christmas Carol* by Charles Dickens in which he aims to convince the reader that Marley is dead. Witness there, along with the author's genuine respect for tradition, the craft of a master wordsmith:

> Old Marley was dead as a door-nail. Mind, I don't mean to say that I know of my own knowledge what there is particularly dead about a door-nail. I might have been inclined, myself, to regard a coffin-nail as the deadest piece of ironmongery in the trade. But the wisdom of our ancestors is in the simile, and my unhallowed hands shall not disturb it or the country's done for (Dickens 2009, 1).

The snippets of thought that constitute someone's stream of consciousness cannot hold a candle to the patience of a long sentence.

The masterpieces of old succeed in conveying the most profound levels of meaning from the artist to his audience. In that connection, we must hope, lies the aesthetic of the future. Such a connection, the successful communication with an audience, realizes the inherent beauty of the human soul. That is how we recognize a master: he speaks to each and all in a language we know and understand.

THE PIANO TEACHER

- *A Humble Account* -

A close friend who spent more than three decades teaching piano privately granted me the following interview. Her firsthand account, in defense of the preceding essay on modernism, offers evidence to substantiate my view of its cultural effects upon the music world. Honoring her condition of anonymity, I use only initials.

WGC: First, let me thank you most sincerely for taking the time to share your long experience as a piano teacher.

ACM: My pleasure, certainly.

WGC: You grew up in America and started learning piano in the 1950s. What were piano lessons like in those days?

ACM: My family lived in a subdivision of postwar bungalows, and at that time, there was a piano teacher in nearly every neighborhood. She was the woman who could play piano and brought in a little extra family income by giving lessons to neighborhood children after school. Many homes at the time had an old piano in the living room, an upright, badly out of tune, and it seemed only proper that at least one child should learn to play. The teacher was a wife, mother, and homemaker who would serve her own baked goods at recitals held at the local church. It was a humdrum sort of activity—piano teaching—stereotyped as dull, boring.

WGC: In our conversations over the years, I seem to recall a few choice anecdotes from your career that might dispel that impression, especially involving students who did not come willingly to lessons.

ACM: I had many of those but only a few who were creative in acting out. There was one little man, quietly disdainful, who tried spooning chocolate pudding into my mailbox, thinking I would mistake it for a reeking pile of something unpleasant. Of course, it did not reek. He may have been the same one who carved an obscenity into a wooden walking stick that stood in the umbrella stand, but I could not be sure.

WGC: What about the girls?

ACM: They were more well behaved, but there was an awkward situation when one little girl snuck into an upstairs bedroom and pilfered a plush toy cat. Among the older students, one girl came to her lesson overheated after a basketball game and suddenly had to race to the powder room, where she vomited in and around the commode. Extremely embarrassed, she offered to clean it up, but I sent her home and used up a roll of paper towels.

WGC: Your house had the perfect layout for a piano teacher: a small library for the studio, the wide hallway from the front door with bench and chairs where students and parents could wait, and the powder room just outside the studio.

ACM: The floor plan was a major selling point of the house, which served me well. I remember one time when the little sister of my student—quite young, not old enough for lessons—was sitting in the hall alone. She went into the powder room, where I kept by the sink a dish with small souvenir soaps collected from various fancy hotels in the area. I later discovered to my chagrin that the child had very helpfully *unwrapped* them!

WGC: So much for five-star hotels! What was the demographic of your clients?

ACM: Well, as to that, most of my students were of course simply average children whose parents could afford or had inherited a piano of some kind and wanted their progeny to have a passing acquaintance with music, and the piano is a good way to achieve this at a young age. At the height of my career, I had almost forty pupils in thirty- or forty-five-minute weekly lessons, taught after school. I myself was younger than most piano teachers and had never attended a conservatory, but I held a bachelor's degree in music education with piano as my instrument.

WGC: How would you compare your teaching career with your childhood experience learning piano?

ACM: I fully expected, when I opened a piano studio, to replicate that experience of lessons as a child in a small suburban town where all the streets were named for trees: the piano teacher was on Willow Street, the doctor on Maple, the dentist on Elm. My teacher had her piano in a small room off the living room. I took to it naturally and learned very quickly. I barely saw the teacher sitting behind me to the extent that I could not tell you what she looked like. The music was my motivation; I simply loved it and needed no prodding to practice.

When I began my career, piano teaching was not drastically different than it had been in my student days, but I did not realize that I started teaching when the profession—and classical piano music as a genre—began a long decline. I distributed flyers in the neighborhood, advertised in local papers, and was eager to take on students of all kinds. For the first decade or so, mine was an evangelical approach. Those students who had no gift or who did not practice, I reasoned, might at least acquire an appreciation for classical music.

WGC: Did you succeed?

ACM: Honestly, my zeal was not infectious. A good percentage of my students would take lessons for a year or two and then drop out. These failures, while frustrating, could as easily be laid to my ineptitude as to their inability, but when I joined a local piano teachers' association, I realized the scope of these conditions. Even the best-trained, experienced teachers shared the same problems, which would be discussed and lamented at meetings. Parents would reveal their ignorance by inquiring whether they really needed to have a piano at home or if an electronic keyboard would do. The piano is difficult to learn and harder still if one cannot even enjoy the sound of the instrument, and motivation is key. But of course, an out-of-tune spinet in the basement is not exactly motivating either.

WGC: You have often spoken of your role in the piano teachers' association, where I recall you were the group secretary for some years before retiring. Would you describe for me what their meetings were like?

ACM: Yes, well, there were three or four meetings in the academic year, always on a Friday morning with members hosting. Typically, only about half of the fifteen members would attend. The fall meeting would take place at the home of the president, who prepared the dining room table with coffee and tea, pastry, fruit, crackers and brie, decorating it with crepe paper pumpkins and tissue paper autumn leaves. When the meeting was called to order, the ladies would take their tea or coffee to the living room. After the reading of the minutes and a treasurer's report, the business at hand invariably revolved around their joint recitals and where to hold them.

WGC: Might I ask what was your assessment of fellow piano teachers?

ACM: Frankly, as I sat through several of these meetings a year, I developed the conviction that piano teachers are to a great extent savants. Naturally, they are excellent pianists, but other than piano music, their thinking, in my opinion, is unfortunately blinkered. They would show scant curiosity, for example, as to the historical root of their problems.

WGC: Surely you would have discussed the common difficulties of the profession in your meetings.

ACM: Oh, indeed so. The appeal of classical music had dwindled in our time. Students and even their parents were not exposed to it and had no taste for it. Aside from Asian immigrants, who retained some tradition of discipline, piano pupils did not practice routinely and so did not learn to play. We often complained that their only true and universal passion was team sports. They took piano lessons only to strengthen a college application.

WGC: What about teaching techniques and strategies? Did such topics come up?

ACM: Of course, we would spend some time swapping ideas and especially tactics or repertoire to motivate students. Sports became a growing issue, taking over the after-school hours, with parents as ardent as their children. What was left of an evening gradually became filled by homework. There was barely time in a week to squeeze in a half-hour piano lesson let alone daily practice. Increasingly it was sports that dominated: soccer in the fall and spring, basketball in winter. Even dainty, slight girls wanted to emulate tall black men.

WGC: You and I have often puzzled over the popularity of soccer.

ACM: Yes. As you know, I used to chide my students about soccer especially because of heading the ball, and this was many years before the ill effects of chronic exposure to contrecoup injury began to raise concern. The brightest boy I ever taught was smart enough not to play soccer, and his parents, both with doctorates from Stanford, were in agreement. On the other hand, a very promising girl I had later in my career led me to retire. Her mother was of Polish descent, and the Poles have a wonderful musical heritage. This girl was learning quickly and, even more unusual, showing enthusiasm for the piano repertoire. After two years of lessons, she quit to play basketball. That did it for me. When even a child who enthused over the music of Chopin could give it up for hoop dreams, it was time to see the handwriting on the wall.

WGC: With the declining appreciation of classical music, I am sure it was difficult to find appropriate student repertoire.

ACM: Exactly. At our teachers' meetings, we often opined that we were swimming against the tide, particularly with respect to repertoire. It was the guitar that reigned supreme, not piano. Reluctant piano students would bring in keyboard arrangements of popular rock-style pieces they had found at the music store, hoping thereby to make lessons more palatable, but the piano is not a guitar. Every instrument has its own idioms, and attempts to notate rhythmic riffs improvised by a rock group produced sheet music that would be completely unplayable.

As years went by, even the parents of my students would be totally unfamiliar with the classical style and appeal to me to teach something more popular. In such cases, I was grateful for Disney productions, because from these there would always be student-level versions of tuneful songs. Otherwise, popular music had by then degraded into a kind of three-note incantation, a high-decibel, profane plainsong.

WGC: Fittingly, if you recall, Gregorian chant became trendy some years ago. To anyone who loves classical music, it must seem unfathomable that most people do not find it beautiful but old, musty, and irrelevant, though some seem to acquire a taste for it when they themselves fit that description.

ACM: Well said, my friend! The problem as I see it, and I know you agree, is that any serious music written after the turn of the twentieth century has been avant-garde, and the musical establishment of academia, orchestras, and impresarios will never stop trying to foist it upon the paying public. I blame the declining interest in classical music and the now nearly universal ignorance of it on this unfortunate history, because the old chestnuts of the classical repertoire have no modern parallels.

WGC: How did your fellow piano teachers deal with this disinterest in classical music? Did they attempt to introduce students to more modern styles?

ACM: My colleagues, considering themselves part of the establishment, would dutifully endeavor to introduce modern composers to students—Bartok, Tcherepnin, Satie, as the more acceptable examples—and often met resistance from children who never wanted piano lessons in the first place. In our meetings, they would listen politely to my perspective on the role of the avant-garde and its atonal revolution but clearly accepted the idea that the tonality that was our centuries-old heritage could not be expected to have survived another one, regardless of how ugly the consequences.

WGC: Over the years, you and I often discussed the glaring need to promote the knowledge of music fundamentals or what is referred to as music theory, essentially the grammar of our music language. Can you explain your keen interest in the subject?

ACM: Since early childhood, I have found music intensely moving, and as I know you are aware, it is referred to as the language of the emotions. When I began studying music, I became curious to learn just why and how it can be so emotional. Music theory tells us how music is constructed and, with historical reference points, gives clues to its seemingly magical powers.

WGC: Can you give an example?

ACM: You yourself provided one just recently.

WGC: Ah, yes! The eleventh of the "Hungarian Dances" of Brahms, which I heard on the radio and was bewitched.

ACM: It is extremely evocative, wailing in deep sorrow and pain, then subsiding in consolation. From his early years, Brahms was enamored of the gypsy style. I took out a copy of it to analyze the harmonies. As one expects, there are eight bars in a minor key followed by eight in the major; however, the harmonic progressions are unusual. He does not go to the relative major but uses a neighbor dominant to lead us far afield—in just two phrases! This sort of balance between familiarity and surprise is often what our brains react to.

WGC: Music theory was always a priority in your teaching. Did you see this emphasis as one way to save the glorious traditions of Western music from the devastation of modernism?

ACM: Oh yes, and at the same time, I recognized an obvious bias on the part of teachers in favor of performance, making music theory the stepchild of music education. Of course, I hoped at least some few of my students might carry forth an interest in the subject. I had been teaching for ten years when I took on an active role in helping to create a music theory program for the teachers' association. Shortly thereafter, I started a private effort to promote music theory instruction as a sideline to piano teaching.

WGC: That was quite an innovative program, as I recall. When did you begin it?

ACM: It was in 1985 with a Mac Plus computer and appropriate music notation software. The program provided music teachers with annual music theory examinations by mail order. In a few years, it grew to a seven-level course including student workbooks and an honor roll with special engraved awards. With my own students, I preached the value of the scale not only as a useful technical exercise but as the basis of our unique music language. Anyone who stayed with me until high school graduation received a gift of my favorite book on the subject, *Music, the Brain, and Ecstasy* by Robert Jourdain.

WGC: You gave me my copy of that informative book. Jourdain makes the most striking observation, which few people appreciate, that the scale upon which Western music was historically based has an ideal number of notes, giving composers inexhaustible opportunities, unlike the music of any other culture.

ACM: The book is really very instructive about the Pythagorean scale, but you would be surprised how many adults who engage me in discussion, even those with higher degrees, have never heard of it or the role of Pythagoras, who based the scale on the acoustical phenomenon of the harmonic series. Interestingly, when composers abandoned this scale, they alienated the lay audience that was ignorant of it as the soul of the music they loved. The masses then turned to untutored musicians who produced music of throbbing rhythm but fewer notes and then predictably no tones at all—rap music. Rhythmic speech.

WGC: No doubt the tides you swam against got steadily stronger.

ACM: They did indeed, and slowly they even changed in color. Our local group had started as a coffee klatch for a few Anglo-Saxon ladies who gave piano lessons to the neighborhood children. Gradually, we were accepting Asian and Russian teachers as members. They came highly qualified, especially the Russians, many of whom trained at the Moscow Conservatory and were accustomed to daily, not weekly, lessons. They would express their horror at the much lower standards here in their new country. Piano students also slowly became majority Asian. The Smiths and Joneses, the Cohens and Bernsteins, gave way to Nguyen, Wang, Liu, Zhou, and then Gupta and Singh.

WGC: Globalization brought immigrants from the world over to America, but surely it was curious that these particular groups gravitated to the study of classical piano. How would you explain it?

ACM: My theory is that modernism was regarded as decadent in the authoritarian regimes of the East, which were cultural backwaters where traditional arts lingered. For example, Russia had a glorious musical heritage that the Soviets continued to promote, so when the USSR broke up, musicians who emigrated demonstrated superior training. The isolation of China for so long by a brutal ideology likewise prevented the influence of the avant-garde. When the Peoples' Republic began to open up, the Western musical classics were still appreciated even more than folk styles.

WGC: We see this shift among talented performers as well, do we not—pianist Lang Lang and cellist Yo-Yo Ma as two examples.

ACM: Quite so. Nonetheless, even this new contingent continues to play the old repertoire, which are undoubtedly masterpieces. Contemporary composers who want to write tonal music are shut out. Their options are Hollywood or Broadway.

WGC: There is widespread hunger for approachable music written in a language the beauty and meaning of which are universally understood.

ACM: Exactly. Just look at the enormous success of Briton Andrew Lloyd Webber with his soaring melodies. Today, however, a serious work such as a symphony, composed in the tradition of tonal music, is unacceptable to orchestras, institutions, and critics, who regard only atonality as legitimate, ostensibly convinced that in some far-off century, the average listener will grow to admire it. These staunch holdouts for the avant-garde disdain popularity anyway.

WGC: You have yourself published teaching pieces for piano, I believe.

ACM: I was in fact fortunate enough to have published two collections for piano students. There is that one mode still available for tonal composition, and that is at the student level. The implication of this very fact is an ironic vindication of tonality: it appeals to children who will accept nothing else. My setting of the *Rubaiyat*, however, for piano, chorus, and baritone solo, composed when I was in my thirties, still languishes in the piano bench.

WGC: Most unfortunate! Did you make any other forays as a composer early in your career?

ACM: Once. There was another ladies group in my community that was considered very elite; its members were skilled pianists who met once a week to perform for one another. They also admitted composers. When I attended a meeting as a guest, a beautiful, traditional piece written by a member was on the program, and I was encouraged to apply for membership, submitting manuscripts in various styles, one of which was required to be modern. In that latter category, I chose a song I wrote that sounded contemporary, but I could not bring myself to capitulate with atonality. Of course, I was rejected with the comment that I wrote "as though the twentieth century never happened." I took it as a compliment, but this was a personal example of how the composer of tonal music is denied cultural influence.

WGC: You kept directing the music theory program even after you retired from teaching piano. Did you witness the same trends in the theory program that you saw in piano teaching?

ACM: Over the years, yes—more Asian and Russian teachers and considerably more Asian names on the honor roll. The client base also grew older and the orders smaller, though most teachers would hold on even with just a few students—a little extra money in their twilight years. No longer is there a piano teacher in every neighborhood, nor is every living room graced with an old upright.

WGC: As a music lover myself, I understand your nostalgia.

ACM: I know you do. I loved my first piano, which took up half of the living room in our family's modest house. It was tall with a mirror across the top section and above the fall-board the obscure name "Montague E. Marks." To a child's ears, this instrument had a magical sound, and very soon I was playing it with hands together, making those simple harmonies contained in the first piece of the John Thompson First Grade Book, having the words "Off I go to music land." I used that same book in teaching beginners for many years, and I enjoyed sharing my love of music with children. I had no children of my own and would joke that I had the advantage of sending them home to their weary parents after thirty minutes.

WGC: As the crop of students became less disciplined or interested, why did you continue?

ACM: I rationalized that they might come to appreciate classical music and acquire some knowledge of it. At my semi-annual recitals, which I eventually began to hold in my living room on an excellent Steinway piano, the growing need to apologize and excuse the poor performance of students became a pitiful embarrassment. It was time to stop swimming against the tide.

WGC: So you did. You retired from piano teaching earlier than most.

ACM: I might have continued, but the trajectory of the profession continued inexorably in one direction. Students, even those with a knack for the instrument, gave up after a year or two to play basketball, and if a child was not talented, the family would see no point in continuing. The love of making music was not a good enough reason.

WGC: Have many colleagues in the teachers' group retired?

ACM: No, they continue on, finding the occasional Chinese child with a gift—and a tiger mom—to learn the standard repertoire quickly and play it with great skill. Occasionally I still attend a meeting, smiling quietly as they talk ad infinitum about where to hold their next recital. Their profession is dwindling, piano sales decline, and students drop out while they as teachers miss the big picture. The repertoire they teach year after year is stale, and they scratch their heads in the vain effort to understand why their students prefer to learn piano versions of monotone pop songs written for guitar.

WGC: Well, as long as there are Asians who remain uncorrupted by sports mania or rock star fandom, classical piano music from the three centuries of its historic heyday will occupy a cultural niche, albeit shrinking.

ACM: That is the truth, and I retain a glimmer of hope that archeologists in a far-distant future will unearth buried manuscripts left by those unsung composers of our day who were never allowed a hearing.

WGC: I wonder, given a chance, what a contemporary person inclined to perpetuate the traditional language of our musical heritage might compose. More likely, any musician so inclined has been retrained in cybernetics.

ACM: You and I have observed that due to the absence of new tonal music, serious musicians appear to be delving into archives of prior centuries for neglected works by famous composers or the works of those less known. This is particularly obvious on the few remaining classical music radio stations, the ones that depend for survival on a shrinking fan base. I even conjecture that a living composer, wanting to create tonal music and have it performed, might try to present his work as a long-lost piece by one of the three Bs—Bach, Beethoven, or Brahms—recently discovered in the attic of an old music shop in Vienna!

In my old studio, I now have a recliner by the window facing south that affords an excellent view of the early sunsets in winter. Symbolic, perhaps: the sunset of my life, of piano music, and of the piano teacher.

WGC: Thank you again, my friend, for your insights and your contributions to music education. May you enjoy many more years of peaceful sunsets!

THE REIGN OF SPORT

- Bread and Circuses -

I must attest to the passion for sport that is centuries old in my native England, particularly for what we call football, known in the States as soccer. This passion became official with the founding of the Football Association in 1863, reaching a fever pitch a hundred years later with the rise of hooliganism. Brawls were breaking out at the games between fans of the opposing teams, referred to then as "football hooligans." The fights were so rabid and became so common that the phenomenon was dubbed the "English disease" before it was checked. That said, our fanaticism for sport cannot rival that seen in America, where it has been compared with ancient Rome in its era of empire, when according to the poet Juvenal, the Pax Romana was ensured by giving the masses their "bread and circuses" and sacrificing the gladiators. Football players in this analogy are the gladiators of the Pax Americana. Trained in college teams, which once embodied the nostalgic experiences of higher education but are now simply the minor leagues, these athletes are revered by one and all. What long ago was a game with which we entertained ourselves on chilly autumn weekends has become much more: a significant source of revenue for many schools and the perpetual preoccupation of millions of fans. In this trend, football in America has been joined by all other professional sports.

I have spent a good deal of my adult years in the States, more than enough to be dismayed by the excessive enthusiasm for the games. Irritation does not take long to set in, given the considerable fuss and bother of intense fans. There is nothing inherently bad about sporting activities. They are generally healthful and entertaining to watch, at the same time promoting esprit de corps in society. The point I make is that when a thing is taken to the extreme, bad things happen, personally and socially. Empires fall.

For example, because of the obsession with sport, an incalculable stream of wealth flows toward the sector, and countless children dream of entering it. For African Americans, sport is key to escaping the ghetto whether in boxing, paramount for generations, or now basketball, fortunately less injurious. For weightless young girls who can balance on a beam and somersault through the air, gymnastics is the magic carpet to fame and fortune. The wealth is so vast that it spills over onto adjunctive enterprises: the colleges, media, team owners, sportswear makers, shoemakers, "doctors, lawyers, and Indian chiefs" no doubt. So much wealth is involved that entire cities remake themselves panning for Olympic gold, sprouting excessive numbers of stadia like so many municipal warts. As for the athletes, a relative few, gleaned by fate from millions of aspirants, are awarded tens of millions of dollars by persons who are competing for the privilege of heaping this largesse. Cities will bid millions and manipulate the rules to obtain a coveted player, and the absurd fact about such absurdity is that no one finds it absurd.

The commercialization of sport, with players bearing corporate logos and fans wearing expensive, team-branded shirts, hats, or shoes, is the inevitable result of a torrential cash flow that originates in the wallets of hundreds of millions of the sports crazed. They will sacrifice, they will pay, but how has it come to this and why?

Consider the United States, where the phenomenon is most visible. In 1957, when the Russians launched the first manmade satellite, Sputnik, into orbit around the Earth, it was a deep shock to the American sense of scientific hegemony. President Eisenhower declared that the nation must catch up. Math and science departments throughout the educational system went into high gear. When John F. Kennedy was elected, he jumped on the bandwagon with his famous commitment to the space program, namely a moon landing. By the early 1960s, SAT scores were at an all-time high. At the same time Kennedy was determining to put a man on the moon, he noted as a curious aside the declining physical fitness of American youth. To remedy this condition, he established the President's Physical Fitness Program, and from this small beginning, the term fitness grew to be the watchword of our time.

There is nothing unworthy about physical fitness; it is an admirable enough goal. The trouble is that children are already full of energy and eager to be active; it is the quiet pursuits—reading, studying, or practicing a musical instrument—in which they need encouragement. Announcing that they will be required to attain physical fitness is like threatening to throw Br'er Rabbit into the briar patch. What a grand, lofty rationale for neglecting one's homework—and so they did.

Over the years, a generation raised in the worship of fitness became parents themselves, bringing to their children's schools and Little Leagues their intense fanaticism. Sports in the schools began to have priority over all else: the arts, considered the most dispensable, and even the raison d'être of education, academics. Students with the ability to win in the games came to know that they would receive qualifying grades, like so many laurel leaves, without their needing to study or learn a thing.

In the normal course of our lives, before we become debilitated by age, physical activity is so easy that we take it for granted. To walk, bend, lift, or move in whatever manner is automatic, not requiring much conscious thought. Mental activity is much more difficult, demanding that we discipline and organize our normally haphazard train of thought. For sports to become predominant over academics with but slight provocation is not surprising. The body wins handily over the mind as the ready source of the most gratification.

Moreover, the highest achievements in athletics involve the added facility of predetermination. If you were born to be taller than average, you will be good at reaching a hoop to put a ball through it; if you tend to be hefty, you will not find it hard to carry a football down the field in the face of opposition. Athletes who excel are born to do so to a large extent. In the realm of intellect, while the truly greats—the Einsteins—may be inherently so, there is a considerable area of leeway where individual effort can effect meaningful improvement. If you study hard, you can learn more math, but no amount of practice will make you taller, and nothing short of steroids will turn an ectomorph into a mesomorph.

In athletics, there is, with rare exception, a natural-born elite, a coterie of the physically well endowed who happen of be tall enough, strong enough, heavy enough, or light enough as the particular game demands. Toward this group flow wealth and celebrity without the benefit of credentials save their genes. The consequence, as with any elite born to power and especially in this case involving physical power, is arrogance and a growing abuse of that power. As the roster of athletes who rape and abuse grows longer, it is exceeded by the numbers of fans who do likewise, especially as has been shown during the broadcast of major sporting events. Shockingly yet increasingly, a subliminal undercurrent makes it acceptable to believe that might makes right, giving the right to mistreat and even injure any person one can overpower. The preeminence of sport as it permeates our society degrades our culture.

In professional sports, the race card is more like a wild card, especially in America. It appears that the world of sports in recent decades has served African Americans as an avenue of redress. Millionaire athletes can at last avail themselves of a prestige and influence denied them in other walks of life, making up for centuries of deprivation and exploitation. The money itself would seem to refute any suggestion that black athletes are exploited, as in the bad old days when, for example, a prize fighter would put his health on the line only to be cheated of his purse. Now the Reebok is on the other foot—or is it?

For every millionaire basketball player, how many millions of young black men succumb to the lure of the NBA while dashing any realistic hope of an MBA? They are exploited by the hoop dream. In a perverse way, the superstars are still being exploited, mostly by white owners and managers vying to throw money at them in a peculiar new form of potlatch. How long will it be before none but the richest fans can afford a ticket to sporting events? Already these spectacles are becoming the preserve of the mostly white upper crust in their sky boxes with the black superstar athlete, a living lawn jockey, bought and paid for. The new patronage system of slavery has black and white locked in mutual exploitation.

Even in golf, the sport of the country club, young prodigy Tiger Woods saw fit to sacrifice his last two years at Stanford for the opportunity to beat the white man at his own game. What, after all, has higher education to offer? What are literature, history, and the great philosophies of humankind next to the PGA tour? Still, to give the sport its due, it is the last bastion of the true gentleman, surprisingly I daresay, given its origins in medieval Scotland. The vagaries of the game, unlike any other—the weather, turf, hazards, and even the rim of the cup—imbue its practitioner with humility. When the most accomplished golfer can have bad luck, no one can afford arrogance. Furthermore, golf has as its object the noncompetitive goal of manipulating a small ball into a small hole hundreds of yards away. Each player strives in this common direction. By contrast, many of the most popular games today have the principal aim of impeding one's opponent.

In tennis, one might be forgiven for imagining that the pleasurable part of the activity lies in maintaining a consistent volley of the ball across the net, in which aim the players would need to cooperate. One would be dreaming. Poles away from such cooperation, the name of the game is to make your opponent miss. To win, in other words, you must seek to make your partner fail. All in good fun.

Even in baseball, a national pastime in the States, the pitcher is given the convoluted assignment of throwing the ball into an area where the batter could hit it but in such a way as to give him great difficulty in doing so. Do we want the ball to be hit or not? If so, why not give the batter a good shot at it? No, the real goal, appearances aside, is to make him miss. The pitcher only seems to be throwing a ball for the batter to hit when in truth he intends for the batter to fail.

American football may have superseded baseball as the national pastime and assuredly as the national religion. It is blatantly and openly obstructionist, with two teams plunging toward their goal against the determined blockade of the other and more like warfare than any other sports. The popularity of the game forces us to wonder if it is serving to ventilate our collective aggressiveness in the absence of war. If we are warlike by nature, if it is in our genes, perhaps we should bless football as a relatively benign, nonfatal alternative expression of this tendency.

Over the years, as these gladiators have become larger and heavier, indisputable evidence has amassed that traumatic brain injury (TBI) is caused by careers of repeated concussions. The response has been for players to demand monetary restitution, at least for the family that survives their abbreviated lives. There comes the call for better helmets as though, upon the onslaught of a several-hundred-pound opponent, any shell might prevent the brain from crashing against the skull. The idea of such a magic helmet gives parents the vain hope that their young sons may continue to engage in their most beloved activity in safety, though a younger generation is reluctantly seeing the light, at least when it comes to the brains of their children. Slowly, football is declining in popularity, overtaken it seems by basketball and hockey.

As the predominant ethos becomes competition, not cooperation, and competition of a personal and destructive kind, we must again note that the pervasiveness of sports transmutes the social fabric, coarsening it. There is no difference between the tennis player bent on foiling his opponent and the freeway driver determined to let no car in front of him if he can prevent it—no difference between the pitcher hurling a fast ball for the batter to miss and the bureaucrat sabotaging a coworker to make himself look good, the linebacker driving through a wall of bodies to advance the ball at all cost, and the woman with the grocery cart ramming the heels of her fellow shoppers at every turn in her passion to reach the checkout counter.

Other factors are at work making society more competitive: the state of the economy and the sheer size of the population. In defense of team sports, there is that esprit de corps they create. But I would submit that team spirit is a tribal passion, which in its full fury may be the worst enemy of civilized society. The football hooligans made that case.

Further implications, social and economic, relate to the emphasis on physical pursuits to the disdain and neglect of the mental. Raised in a society that grants its most acute attention and serious regard to sports tournaments—the World Cup, Super Bowl, World Series, NBA, and Stanley Cup playoffs—children can be forgiven for noticing that everything else—reading, math, history, and art—pales in importance. They can be forgiven for assuming that the ability to dribble a ball down the court is more critical than the ability to do simple arithmetic. When they are handed their diploma, having put in years of schooling only to emerge illiterate and unschooled, they should be forgiven for not giving a damn. They have been instilled with a belief that life is all about the games, and all that matters is that we play, that we revel in the exertion of physical power.

What happens to productivity when this new generation, ignorant of basic skills, enters a demanding job market? Some will flounder and lapse into bitter resentment at the expectations. Our schools and universities continue to turn out many highly competent, motivated graduates, thanks to whom society continues to function—so far. However, there are the horror stories: 911

emergency operators who fall asleep on the job, nurses who give the wrong medication or dose, bank clerks who make errors in accounts or credit records, and mail carriers who throw the mail away rather than deliver it. To blame these on the popularity of sports is perhaps to stretch a point beyond all reason, yet consider the odd game, itself beyond reason, that is the most popular in the world: soccer.

In spite of the fact that *Homo sapiens* has gained immense evolutionary advantage from the opposable thumb or that all the artifacts of civilization past and present derive from the superior human brain, this preeminent world sport precludes the use of the hands while endangering the brain by heading of the ball. The human hand is undoubtedly a masterpiece of creation. With it, you can write, sculpt, play a musical instrument, perform surgery, and build a house, skyscraper, car, or airplane. Picture a world in which a generation or two of children have grown up pursuing an athletic activity that forbids the use of their hands. Is it such a stretch to imagine that more than several of these people will have no interest in creative arts or even the activities of gainful employment?

There is no stronger evidence that professional sports occupy a position of imperium in modern society than the cruel fate of the variety show that, until the later years of the last century, offered pure entertainment on television. On these programs, performers would dance, sing together or solo, and do magic tricks or stand-up comedy for our pleasure. Even figure skating was televised as an entertainment. To generations who grew up awarded a plethora of trophies for participation if nothing else, all that seemed pointless. Now there must be a panel of judges making comments and picking winners in a season-long tournament of elimination. Risibly, at least one judge must have a British accent. Does the audience assume that Brits have better judgment than others?

For all the bread and circuses, Roman society declined, weakened, and succumbed to the barbarians. If the games are just games, producing only entertainment, we should acknowledge that truth lest we meet the same fate. On the other hand, if they fill a role as mock warfare and do so adequately, that may be the saving grace. The international Olympic Games might in some sense be viewed as channeling our innate territorial imperative, thus tempering our proclivity for tribal hostility. We would need only remember in our frenzy for the home team that *games are only games!*

APPEARANCE AND RELITY

- If the Shoe Fits -

My younger sister wrote to me many years ago with the following boast: "Although I was born in 1947, I have never worn, have never owned, have never succumbed to that fashion imperative, blue jeans. I pride myself in being one of but three known females who can make this claim, along with a cousin and a friend of mine. When my ancient mother-in-law appeared in designer jeans just lately, I suddenly knew I would have no trouble retaining my status!" And that she has to this day, some time since the cousin and mother-in-law passed to their reward—variously dressed, I suppose—while that fashion imperative remains alive and well.

Jeans, not always blue, were once known by their more descriptive name dungarees and were worn for farm work, including shoveling the dung of livestock. Now fashion designers fix their names to the back pocket while exacting handsome prices for them from deeper ones. The style is so ubiquitous that extraterrestrials might be excused for deciding that the whole world has joined a global collective farm where this is the only permissible article of clothing for every man, woman, child, and old person. It is required after all for mothers, teachers, executives on Casual Fridays, and on and on. They all have so much manure to shovel—everyone except my sister and her friend, above mentioned.

While I do not shovel manure, I often wear jeans at the family farm in England. I do not find them attractive, but irrespective of how I appear in them, they are practical work clothes. Regardless, as I begin this essay, let me hasten to clarify that the matter of delineating appearances from reality is discussed here at a superficial level, the strata at which we all endeavor to interact and as best we can to disentangle the knots of our karma. Reality is many layered, from the microscopic to the astronomic, and much more profound when we dig for the roots of the human experience. Nonetheless, I lay out certain of my opinions on the subject, typically seditious.

Appearances are deceiving, as they say. My physician, who makes a better-than-average income, studiously avoids all symbols of status or wealth. He wears a cheap watch and drives any of several old jalopies he keeps on hand. I have cajoled him more than once that his carefully maintained slovenliness is as pretentious as the fastidious appearance of the status seeker with his Mercedes and Rolex. It is the other side of one coin. Each side credits the value of the tender; certain material items, whether coveted or rejected, are agreed-upon symbols.

I once read a newspaper article in which the reporter had a conversation with a group of African American boys on the street corner. They were dressed in the uniform of the "hood," conveying the tough, "gangsta" look. In speaking with them, this writer found them to be ordinary teenagers with the normal concerns and ambitions—polite, intelligent. How curious that they wanted others to see them as so different from their real natures.

Appearances *are* deceiving and calculated to be so: "Just because I dress like a ghetto drug dealer doesn't mean you should jump to conclusions." "I may not look like a doctor, but I play one in real life." "You probably thought from my attire that I'm a farmhand, but I'm a dignified old lady."

This sort of pure mischief tends to be harmless, an attempt to tweak the sensibilities of others thought to be staid or biased. It introduces some amusing uncertainty into the business of assessing those who cross our path, a dab of cognitive dissonance as sauce to the salad of our acquaintanceships. The perpetrators want us to know that appearance is not reality and should not be taken as such, that we should always be ready and willing to delve beneath the surface to find the genuine, that we should not judge a book by its cover. To this I retort if the shoe fits, be prepared to wear it.

When nearly every living soul has joined into this kind of deception and it has gone on for generations, appearance has a way of becoming reality. We come to perceive a world without dignified old ladies, without respectable physicians, and with no black youth capable of anything but crime, though we know it isn't so. When they themselves have said it is for so long, we come to believe it. Appearance is our first take on reality, the initial aspect of reality, and so even as it deceives, it is real. At the level of perception, you are whatever you pretend to be; that is face value, and we should always be prepared to be taken at face value. You cannot set out to fool the public only to object when you succeed.

In many cases, individuals are first fooling themselves. Blue jeans, for example, proclaim that their wearer is free of all formality and considerations of propriety, status, and occupation—that he or she has been liberated into the uniformity of the common man, where comfort is the only measure—except for the label on the back pocket and the faded, torn appearance, which costs extra. Rejecting the old rules, we have codified our own. No white shoes after Labor Day? No footwear except gym shoes.

The notion of ironic self-portrayal embodies our collective insistence on the shocking. Lame as the disguises may be, the intent is to shock or at least disappoint expectations. An old woman in jeans! A doctor wearing a Timex! An honor student dressed like a drug dealer! Is it not the same insistence that relentlessly ups the ante in every arena of our culture? In entertainment, if foul language and intimations of sex and violence no longer shock, we must be more graphic, depict the actual gore and cause regurgitation in paying audiences. In fashion, we must spurn the tameness of grace and beauty to scale the height of ridiculousness and have our sullen models strutting in costumes worthy of science fiction.

Many years ago, the passing of Allen Ginsberg, poet of the Beat Generation, occasioned reminiscences of that movement with its cries for authenticity, its disdain of phoniness. With the old Beatnik gone, is it not time to take another look, to recognize that there is nothing intrinsically authentic about grit, grime, cruelty, and rudeness, that the shiny side of that coin is just as real?

Take our premier status symbol, the automobile. An old Chevy does not impart the stamp of authenticity on someone in the highest tax bracket, who could afford to buy any car, unless he has donated the difference to charity. The same old Chevy is authentic for the person who cannot afford better, and equally authentic is the Jaguar or Mercedes for the wealthy person. He is not a phony unless he stole the car in order to appear wealthy. The fallacy of this old, subversive philosophy is that a lowest common denominator exists among people. Put everyone in a Mao suit, and we are revealed in our commonality. Strip us of all outward signs, and we are equal. The reality is that while we all have much in common as human beings, we are each unique, our differences just as numerous and as valid.

Here we have struck upon the political aspect of appearance. Our jeans and sneakers allow us to display an egalitarian philosophy that we do not practice. Now that this uniform has itself become stratified by status, it is the ultimate hypocrisy, which I fondly hope the next generation will see through. Here we are in our pricey denims appearing to convey that we do not hold ourselves above others, all the while aware that everyone knows we are wearing a status symbol. I say take off the torn, faded things and give them to a poor person! Better still, give him the ridiculous sum you paid for them, and he will feed his family for many months. Virtue does not automatically reside in slovenliness any more than it ever did in neatness. In his quest to stamp out paradox, Western man succeeds only in creating more of it.

How do we find our way through this conundrum of appearance versus reality? Appearance presents us with the reality of what a person truly is or what he has chosen to appear to be, and the latter can be as illuminating as the former. Adolescents adopting the gangster image may be revealing criminal tendencies or the insecurities of their stage in life. Either revelation is equally real. The ubiquitous denim? Much can be learned from this garment. The label tells us a person's annual income, while the lack of a label—combined with torn knees and in the absence of cow manure—indicates a person secure enough not to advertise his financial or social status. The real message of today's jeans and sneakers uniform is the same as the latter-day hoop skirt, bustle, and top hat, i.e., conformity. The vast majority of human beings, guided by their genetic legacy of tribalism, want to belong. Could we not give up the sanctimonious pretext that our mode of dress arises from a political and philosophical superiority to that of our forebears?

Appearance encompasses behavior as well as apparel, and in this social context, it has been disparaged ever since the downfall of the old era of formality when it upheld what subsequent generations saw as a hypocritical society. Behind a facade of gentility, there were plenty of hypocrites who considered it more important to wear the right cravat than to refrain from adultery. Now, while we cannot declare we are better people, we may at least claim to be honest, yet who is the hypocrite if not the teacher pretending to be *cool*, the star athlete pretending to be a student, or the naive suburban teenager pretending to be a prostitute? Worse than hypocrites, these and so many others feel compelled to complain of being misunderstood for the images they have taken such pains to create.

A perfect spoof was the hilarious "Brit-com" from the 1990s, *Keeping Up Appearances,* the BBC series that played upon the timeworn stereotype of the British as pompous snobs. A frumpy, working-class woman, Hyacinth Bucket, played by Patricia Routledge, goes to ridiculously comical lengths trying to keep up the appearance that she is upper class, insisting, for example, that her surname be pronounced "bouquet." Each episode finds her in some farcical situation, often involving loutish family members. One such plot in the first season has the uncouth family following Hyacinth and her long-suffering husband, Roger, to an aristocratic estate. The presence and dowdy *appearance* of these relatives being an insufferable embarrassment, Hyacinth drags Roger around corners and behind hedges in comical attempts to hide from them. Then there is the episode in which Hyacinth has the new vicar come for tea and "light refreshments." After politely correcting the vicar and his wife on the proper pronunciation of her surname, she struggles to fend off her sister and brother-in-law who show up by surprise as always, inappropriately yet in time to spoil the impression she has done her best to create.

The exaggerated swagger of Hyacinth Bouquet is hilarious as she struggles to give a false impression—an aristocratic appearance. On the other hand, might the general adoption of a studied slovenliness these days be a contributing factor to generalized moral laxity, conveying as it does that personal comfort and freedom outweigh all other considerations? Divorce and single-parent families become acceptable, because who needs a father? Why should children dress for school? Let them be comfortable, express their individuality, and practice assertiveness by talking back. We define deviancy down, containing the rising tide of outrageousness by redrawing the coastline of acceptability.

In retrospect, we can see how the social fabric has unraveled as each thread, one by one, is pulled out. If we appear equally at ease and informal, deliberately choosing not to distinguish ourselves through our appearance, should it be a surprise when few of us are accorded dignity and respect—except for those with the proper label on their jeans or the most expensive athletic shoes? The point is how superficial matters can reflect and even influence more profound conditions. Appearance cannot go away; it is the skin upon reality. A response to this realization is the pressure for school uniforms. A uniform removes the distraction of appearance and the comparisons it engenders.

The twentieth century was a time of cultural rebellion. Even before the counterculture of the hippies at whose feet much of the disorder is laid, there were the Beatniks, preceded in turn by the Lost Generation of the Roaring Twenties and the avant-garde. Now that we have passed another *fin de siecle*, the end of an era of upheaval, we would do well to consider appearance and reality. Where is the line now to be drawn?

It would be fine if, in keeping with modern standards of honesty, appearance could coincide precisely and reliably with reality. That would presume that every person is able to perceive and willing to convey reality when there are legions of the confused, delusional, or deceitful. Many people cannot or will not recognize reality, and even among those who do, a large number prefer to dissociate themselves from it deliberately. While there should be no difference between appearance and reality, there is all too often. People are not what they seem to be and do not say what they mean. Rather than revealing reality, like an optical illusion, a *trompe l'oeil*, appearance may conceal it, whether or not as a conscious intention.

Many times when we purport to be brutally, devilishly honest, forgoing the least nod to appearances, we are the ones deluded about reality. In the act of pulling on those jeans to tell the world how casual we are, we only exchange the formality of one costume for the dogmatism of another. We wear our jeans at home, at school, at the office, at the supermarket, or at church, and each place is equated with the others. Parents, children, coworkers, the boss, the reverend minister, friends, and strangers, all in jeans, proclaim themselves equals. A deceitful costume has precluded us from demonstrating that there are places or occasions deserving more respect.

What if we were to be honest? What if we honestly went about seeking the exact correspondence of appearance with reality? Some surprising ironies no doubt would result:

1. "Gangsta" rappers would start behaving like respectable middle-class youth;
2. Parents and teachers would act as though they were older and more experienced than children and dress accordingly;
3. Fashion designers would announce that their shows were nothing but publicity stunts;
4. My physician would stop pretending to be a poor person.

Suffice it to say that if we all came clean and stopped being deceitful, the world would look much different than it does and perhaps more like it once did.

There are instances, however, where common sense may *require* dissembling. Pretending to like your mother-in-law may be hypocritical but pragmatic if you want to stay married. Such small pretensions, once maintained quietly, were considered simple politeness, much as what are now called random acts of kindness were once known as common courtesy. Ideally, we should all be saintly enough to love our enemies, but in lieu of the ideal, it is preferable that we bow to the constraints of civility. Peace is maintained, whereas the indulgence in brutal forthrightness is injurious.

The frank person leaves nothing in question as to his real feelings insofar as he himself is aware of them. At the same time, his rude honesty shows a desire to appear virtuous at the expense of others. There are situations when a spade must be called a spade, yet in small matters, the patient, mature person can keep still out of consideration, that is to say, for the sake of *appearances*. The reality of such a person may include the perspective that politeness is nearly always appropriate and the wisdom that it is almost universally practical. Provoking confrontation to show how honestly you dislike someone does not make you a superior person, only a belligerent fool.

The arcane, stodgy business of etiquette may seem to condone hypocritical pretensions, but it has a defender in Judith Martin of the syndicated Miss Manners column, who points out the vital need for accepted rules. Nowhere is this more ironically underscored than in the mean urban streets where young people kill one another for a certain popular brand of jacket or athletic shoe or upon the perception of being "dissed." The old standards sought to mediate such touchy interactions without violence. If the rules of etiquette have become a life-or-death matter, perhaps the disparagement of *appearances* should be reconsidered.

The intent of so many in manipulating reality is to offend. The media, accosting us relentlessly with the graphic, the gross, the obscene, and the brutal, grab our attention with so-called realism. There are real horrors in this world, but presenting them in living color on a two-story screen in high definition and booming sound track is not reality. Horror is not amusing and should never be invoked to amuse. Leave the hideous crimes to the late-night news and the sexploitation to the world's oldest profession. They do not need to be the staples of our mass culture, but through all of it is our grasping for one another's attention, holding it but momentarily and then ratcheting up the volume. Like an addiction, the compulsion to gain attention falls short, unlike the fulfilling practice of *paying* attention, which is how we learn.

The rapid entrenchment of the internet has brought to the fore this question of distinguishing reality from appearance, since on the frontiers of cyberspace, disinformation undermines all trust that anything is real. Worst of all is the intrusion into the collective psyche, where minds can be manipulated at the behest of despots. There lies serious danger in not knowing what is real: Is there a real ballistic missile on its way from North Korea? Is the Twitter rant about liberal candidates from an unemployed factory worker out on the plains of the Midwestern United States or a Russian internet troll? Are the island nations of the world being swallowed by rising seas, or is that a hoax spread by elitists? The vulnerable will not think to question. As of this writing, there still are trustworthy sources of reliable information; their future is uncertain.

Let me hasten to reiterate that I am referring to that layer of reality at which we live out our lives and, in doing so, must cope with one another on the basis of hard facts mutually acknowledged. Such facts can be cloaked by appearance and appearance taken for reality as when a bright young man with tattoos and piercings is thought to be a hoodlum and turned down for a good job. In generations past, people dressed for the occasion—a job interview, church, school, or work. They dressed to show respect. A vain person might overdress to display superiority, which gave dressing up a bad name, but that is not to say that any effort to be appropriate is vain. Perhaps we may restore some standards of honesty and decency by starting with our own lives, looking honestly in the mirror and asking ourselves with some humility who we are and who we appear to be. With some courage—no longer needing to mislead the world that we have manure to shovel—we might even discard the dungarees.

POTLATCH

- The Culture of Gifts -

Gifts may hold a special place in memories of a happy childhood: the delicious sense of anticipation before Christmas, writing to old Saint Nick with a wish list of toys, trying too hard to sleep on Christmas Eve, barreling down the stairs to a pile of gifts under a glowing and fragrant Scots pine dominating the parlor, the approach of a birthday, looking forward to cake and ice cream, and dropping gift hints to parents and siblings. At my age, I can no longer recapture that childish pleasure or recall with certainty how or when I lost the capacity. I know it has been gone for decades, but whether this result is a matter of age or has derived from other factors would require psychoanalysis. My sister claims that her in-laws have a view toward gifts alien to ours, and while they are Jewish and we are not, this attitude does not relate to ethnicity necessarily. I have had some years to study the question, along with my sister, and it is not surprising that in the course of this compulsory education, the gift has lost its luster for us both. As you may suspect, she put me up to this essay.

My brother-in-law's family is of Eastern European descent, and when it comes to gifts, they maintain a concept of strict reciprocity. To receive a gift is to receive an obligation to match it with precise equivalence. The gift comes to be seen as a burden, and the urge to bestow a gift is inhibited by the fear that it will bring more angst than pleasure. The practice of giving is subverted. If you love someone, you spare him the onus of a gift, while the act of giving a gift becomes a sign of indifference or even hostility.

This attitude is the potlatch culture, and whether it is typical of Eastern Europe, it is not unique in the world. It is often associated with native tribes of the Pacific Northwest in the United States and Canada. Coming from another tradition where a gift is a token of thoughtfulness, expressive of one person's desire to bring pleasure to another, it has always seemed peculiar and paradoxical to me. The failure to give a gift, where I come from, is the sign of indifference. Needless to say, my sister had some period of adjustment before she recognized that her husband's love should be seen in the gifts she *did not* receive. His parents never exchanged gifts, and I observed that he never gave a gift to the person he loved most in life, his grandmother.

Even in our tradition, the one I have always assumed to be mainstream, there is some element of potlatch. This element makes the Christmas holiday unnerving. We search for a thoughtful gift appropriate to the recipient, but complicating the process is the nagging notion that the price tag must be appropriate to that person's role in our life. I may find the perfect tie for my brother except it does not cost enough, or a piece of jewelry may seem too expensive for a cousin. We must add to the equation what the other person gave in past years, and before we know it, a simple purchase has turned into a major quandary. In years past, I have occasionally tried to opt out of the exchange with family members. One year, I made charitable donations in the name of the recipients, and for several years, I used catalogs to send gifts of food, but the rest of the family stuck with tradition, so I am back participating in the insanity.

Insanity is none too strong a word. Even among those of us who give gifts for the pleasure of bringing pleasure, it is the rare gift that succeeds. Mostly we are so myopically self-centered that we select gifts more suitable for ourselves than the recipient or gifts we wish the other person would like or believe he should like, projecting our own tastes and inclination to control, dictate, and manipulate. At Christmas, ghastly sums of money are spent to bestow unwanted material objects that must be returned, exchanged, re-gifted, given to charity, or wasted.

The emotions surrounding a gift change with one's stage of life. As children, being dependents, we covet material things. When we become able to buy these things for ourselves, the gift of them loses importance. It becomes the symbolism of the gift that matters, especially between lovers, where the price of the gift is weighed as an indication of devotion and the remembrance of occasions with a gift becomes critical. Once courtship is over and marital bliss sets in, the meaning of a gift can change again, as we begin to take one another for granted.

There are two sides to this latter circumstance. Some people, like my brother-in-law's family, regard the exchange of gifts between spouses as a foolish gesture demonstrating what ought to go without saying, an unnecessary expenditure. The proof of ongoing devotion, as they see it, is in the fact that these resources are mutual, and the requirement of continual demonstration is insulting. In their tradition, spouses ought to be able take one another for granted as a sign of complete trust. On the other side are those like my sister and me. In more than fifty years of marriage, our parents never failed to exchange birthday, anniversary, and Christmas presents. They believed that it was the thought that counted, the gift signified the thought, and the thought was a reminder of the special regard in which the recipient was held. By the same token, to forget meant that you did not care enough. A major element was the pleasure of giving, carefully choosing a gift and watching it evoke happiness in its receipt. We learned that it was "more blessed to give than to receive" and so are eager to be givers.

This conflict was a struggle for my sister and her husband, but eventually they arrived at common ground. He learned that she expected to be remembered, and she learned to overlook the thoughtless haste of his gift choices. That subjective side will always be missing. She could enjoy giving him a gift, but he will never learn to appreciate one. To him it is a burden, in the potlatch tradition.

The original essence of the Native American potlatch was the demonstration of wealth as measured by how much one could afford to give away. A means of undoing your adversary was to bankrupt him in the obligatory exchange of gifts, but the gift as demonstration has further implications. In a culture where intimate emotions are private, expressing them openly with a gift is distasteful; however, the gift *may* be used to demonstrate emotions that one does *not* feel. In other words, a gift may even be a way to give the false impression of love for someone whom you do not love.

My brother-in-law and his grandmother needed no demonstration of their mutual regard, but he and his mother tended for years to exchange lavish presents implicit with suspicions of insincerity. Theirs was always an ambivalent, problematic relationship.

In my family, a former sister-in-law, who turned out to have serious mental illness, exhibited a peculiar variety of gift behavior. She would insist on the attendance of the extended family at the gift exchange as she opened and flaunted the several extravagant gifts my brother would give her. We would open our inexpensive token gifts. This tableau was enacted at every conceivable occasion; it was like Cinderella's mirror on the wall demonstrating that she was "the fairest of them all." After they had a son, he became the center of the tableau and was given so many presents that he became bored with opening them.

While I can understand these disparate attitudes about giving, I remain in concurrence with the mainstream view, however imperfect it may appear in practice. These other ideas about giving are perversions of a custom that ought to be among the nobler of society. What could be better for children than to learn to think of others in the careful selection and giving of a gift? Who could argue with the nurture of generosity in teaching children to feel pleasure rather than diminishment in bringing happiness to another?

Giving should be available to us as one means of expressing love and regard. We do not need gifts to communicate these feelings; they can be verbalized albeit at the risk of being trivialized like a greeting card. My brother-in-law, when cornered on the subject, always points to the several life insurance policies he maintains, which I am sure my sister finds reassuring. But something may be overlooked, besides one another, in taking each other for granted. What about the survivor? When a person is no longer there to be taken for granted, is there not left a nagging doubt about what mutual feelings were understood or even existed, a doubt that can never be dispelled because there is no one to ask? An occasional reminder in the form of a well-considered gift would one day serve as affirming memory.

Giving in such a true spirit is a difficult, and so a rare, thing. It requires one to purge all notions of potlatch and to think of the other person's needs, desires, tastes, and interests. The old saw about giving something one would himself enjoy receiving is backward. A perfect example is the bottle of French brandy I receive from a colleague each Christmas. He loves brandy and knows I do not. The one person I know who succeeds in the true spirit of giving is a cousin who happens to be a clergyman and so perhaps more prone to think of others. His gifts may vary in value but are always suitable to the recipient, showing the attention he has given to this person and the selection of the gift. I aspire to his example.

No better example exists than "The Gift of the Magi," the well-known short story by William Sydney Porter, known by his pen name O. Henry. Published in 1905, it tells of a young and impecunious couple struggling to find Christmas gifts for one another. Famously, on Christmas Eve, she sells her hair to buy him a watch chain, and he sells his watch to buy her a set of hair combs. With that ironic twist so typical of the author, the real and priceless gift has been the mutual love shown in a willingness to sacrifice.

Those who know my admiration for the Buddhist precepts may be puzzled by this seeming defense of materialism. For them, I must cite one of my favorite Zen stories about a monk who was receiving the great honor of succession from his master, signified by the passing of a treasured book. Thinking himself enlightened, the monk threw the ancient tome into the fire as a demonstration that he understood that material things were insignificant. The master shouted, "What are you doing?" and retrieved the sacred volume from the flames. The monk replied with astonishment, "What are you saying?" Zen is all about paradox. Material things are insignificant and at the same time have meaning to others. Why would one destroy something of such traditional value, showing not his enlightenment but only his lack of respect?

We submit to the culture of potlatch. At that supreme festival of annual giving, Christmas, my sister can expect to receive cheese from our brother in Yorkshire, though she is allergic to dairy products, a sweater from her in-laws, a size too large, representing how she must loom in their lives, and perfume from her husband, because he likes perfume. Not exactly her list to Father Christmas, more on the order of "a partridge in a pear tree." It is enough to elicit a resounding "humbug." Still, she and I cling to the tattered finery of custom, refusing to despair of its redeeming possibility. We try to find just the right gift!

MISOGYNY

- A Modest Proposal -

As I begin this discussion of what is the most pervasive and persistent prejudice of humankind, it is 2019. The last superpower of the latest iteration of civilization is waning under the clumsy governance of a flagrant sexist and notorious womanizer. Overpopulation combined with the superfluity of males and relative paucity of women has led to grotesque sex trafficking. In India, rape is a serious national problem, and in the United States, a third of reported rape cases are solved. A popular series on cable television dramatizes *The Handmaid's Tale,* the dystopian novel by Margaret Atwood that depicts the subjugation of a remnant of fertile women in a future theocracy. The topic of misogyny was never more relevant, but the reams written about it tend to be acrimonious, missing in my view the overarching strangeness of this phenomenon. Let us explore.

Is misogyny uniquely human or held over from protohumans? A social formulation of animal behavior expressed in ways beyond the abilities of any other animal? This would explain why misogyny appears from the dawn of history. In other species that propagate sexually, there is ample evidence, from scientific observation and study, of violent sexual behavior. Even our close primate relatives are guilty. Younger male orangutans are known to force females into copulation, and for this reason among others, the females seek protection of the dominant male. Some species of ducks and geese appear to have violent sexual encounters. The male may get the worst of it in some cases as with cats, where immediately following the act, Tomcat must spring quickly to escape her ferocity. Worse is the case for the male mantis who often falls victim to sexual cannibalism, a practice that gives the name black widow to a certain kind of spider. From the perspective of nature, it would seem that coercion, even violent force, may be a harsh and clumsy fallback method of ensuring species propagation.

We should not, however, conflate sexual violence in animals with hatred. Nearly all other sexually reproducing species are seasonal, and when the season is upon them, both sexes are intent upon engaging in the various ways peculiar to their kind. Misogyny, in contrast, is a *hatred* of the female. I know of no way to detect such an emotion in animals.

We believe ourselves to be above the animals or not animals at all according to fundamentalist religion, though the only thing we may say with certainty about *Homo sapiens* is that he has far more extreme potentiality than any living creature. For example, he is unique in the way he applies that potential to destroying his own kind, where other social species were lucky enough to retain the inhibitions, evolved over eons, against intraspecies killing. How we acquired our destructive characteristics remains a mystery.

In the ancient symbolism, we ate the forbidden fruit from the Tree of Knowledge, and that account of the role of Eve in the Garden of Eden is among the oldest examples of misogyny. Its authors, long before Darwin, discerned that a deal had been made setting us apart, one they described tellingly as a deal with the devil. For the more flexible, liberating ability to learn, humans gave up the constraints of animal instinct. Thus freed, we acknowledge no limits, and combining this freedom with our great cleverness, we exhibit great extremes. The capacity of humankind to invent and the willingness to inflict the most diabolical tortures is staggering. Even to enumerate them preys upon the mind: crucifixion, beheading, the rack, and burning at the stake, to name a few. Any hideous method of torture one could imagine has been perpetrated upon humans by their fellow man, yet that is one end of the polar extreme. At the other we must observe the most lofty ideals, profound philosophies, saintly actions, deep love, and great generosity. The concept of the Great Heart of Compassion in Mahayana Buddhism evinces an extreme emotional capability on the positive end.

We are strange creatures, and perhaps that strange prehistoric prejudice against the female of our kind—once half but an ever-shrinking portion of the entire species—should not surprise us, yet women bear the young and have the larger role in raising them. The bond between mother and child must be strong to see the child through a long phase of dependency. How can it happen that the mothers became a despised category? Does every misogynist hate his mother?

The word *misogyny* comes from the Greek, and many an ancient Greek writer left evidence of harboring the bias. In his work *Politics*, Aristotle wrote of the female being an "incomplete male" and a "deformity." The consensus among the Greeks, as later reported by Cicero, was that misogyny was rooted in a fear of women, an idea far from unusual. Perhaps cruel mothers, terrorizing their sons, are to blame. Jealousy is sometimes offered as another psychological explanation—envy of the ability to give birth. Suffice it to observe that from ancient times, the history of philosophy and literature, not to speak of religion, has seen men openly voicing scorn of the female. An even more obvious, common, and curious sign of misogyny is the f-word, a profanity referring to an act of violent and coercive copulation. Used with such currency, the obscenity sullies a beautiful act of loving intimacy that may express the good that should define humanness. For this reason alone, we must construe that while the word might suggest the sexual behavior of other animals, on the human tongue, its wellspring is hatred, not bestiality.

Judeo-Christian religions have been staunchly patriarchal from their origins, but Islam is the most exacting and rigorous when it comes to subjugating women. The Prophet Muhammad was punctilious in the Koran concerning female modesty, and while most modern followers consider the historical context, radical Islam today seeks a return to the burka and barbaric practices like stoning and beheading. The late H. Patrick Glenn, law professor at McGill University, captured the essence of this Sharia code, describing it as the "concept of mutual obligations of a collective," going on to write that Islamic law "considers individual human rights as disruptive, and justifies the formal inequality of women and non-muslims."[6]

The strange, primitive notions surrounding a woman's hair that Islam harbors to this day are difficult to fathom. Do they consider the sight of it so arousing as to vitiate all self-control in the Islamic male?

We may cede that women have been held back through most of history, politically and socially, by the burdens of child-rearing. Even today the "glass ceiling" looms depending often on the cost or availability of daycare. That division of labor is common to nearly all sexually reproducing animals, but given the extreme social orientation of humans, the absence of women in leadership and professional roles creates a cascade of negative impressions. Uneducated, they are seen as unintelligent; relegated to subservience, they are viewed as submissive. The disparagement of the female becomes so entrenched and pervasive that it ceases to be noticed. The illogic and injustice of misogyny are woven into the social fabric until the most upright men and even women themselves have accepted them.

It is not unusual for individual members of a persecuted minority to internalize self-hatred. In this way, persecution becomes self-perpetuating. Those who are subjected to it are so diminished by it as to represent an affirmation of the bias. In other words, because they have been persecuted, they continue being persecuted. In much of the world, women are not even in the minority, yet the prejudice against them, while subtle and unacknowledged, is strong. The most liberal, seemingly open-minded boss may overlook female employees for promotion or salary increases. Educators, male or female, may assume that girls will never excel in athletics let alone science or math, an idea that becomes self-fulfilling.

---

6. Wikipedia: Sharia. (Glenn, H. Patrick (2014), pp. 199–205.)

As for internalized misogyny, there can be no better example of women's self-hatred than the fashion industry, its long tentacles gripping every aspect of appearance and self-image. Expected to be reed thin, women are driven by male clothing designers into dangerous eating disorders. On the runways, models scowl and strut in bizarre, hideous costumes seemingly intended to humiliate them. The world of high fashion is a professional preserve of gay men, and what can be said of their misogyny, the prevalence of which is anecdotal if not verifiable?

Like racism, misogyny in the age of political correctness is not often expressed openly or blatantly. A noteworthy exception is L. Ron Hubbard, founder of the Church of Scientology, who wrote, "The historian can peg the point where a society begins its sharpest decline at the instant when women begin to take part, on an equal footing with men, in political and business affairs…This is not a sermon on the role or position of women; it is a statement of bald and basic fact."[7] Like nothing else he wrote, this expression of stupidity, bigotry, and sexism broadcasts the simplistic nature of Hubbard's philosophy. Most people who share the sentiment are not so brazen about it and may never have considered themselves prejudiced. Even those who admit to it may be unable to overcome deep-seated attitudes.

Men and women are different, physically and mentally. Their biological roles, through the evolutionary process, have resulted in the distinct agendas elaborated in the first essay of this collection: for the spermatozoa, the wide dispersal of genetic material; for the ova, the nurturance of a limited number of offspring. These differing goals are what we see reflected in gender, the yin and the yang of the Chinese symbol, itself having at times an unfortunate misogynistic connotation. For humans, the unnatural overlay imposed by society allows for the denigration of the female side. A truer perspective on these differences is given by English professors at the University of Southampton, David Glover and Cora Kaplan.

---

7. Wikipedia: Scientology and Gender.

In their book *Genders*,[8] they recount the odd and unnatural views on the subject this way:

> The idea that men and women are more different from one another than either is from anything else must come from something other than nature…Far from being an expression of natural differences, exclusive gender identity is the suppression of natural similarities.

In other words, animals are not burdened by the complex tangle of social expectation and so do not necessarily exhibit such a stark gender dichotomy. The female bear or lion harbors no inhibition about defending herself or her young from a marauding male with all her strength. She does not require self-defense training, never having donned the demureness of femininity that causes the human female to suppress the survival instinct. At the same time, the human male is forced to suppress any show of tenderness—along with his tears.

We are different, but our differences are complementary by nature. They should not lead us to extreme, institutionalized hatred or worse: the wanton and fiendish elimination of female babies, newborn or in utero, because only sons are deemed of value. It is one thing to moderate a burgeoning human population that threatens to overwhelm resources, but where is the logic in eradicating the only members of your kind capable of bearing young? Ask the millions of excess males whose births were welcomed based on a conviction of their disproportionate superiority. Ask them when they have grown to realize the enforced celibacy they are bequeathed. The poor fellows are now referring to themselves as "IC" for involuntary celibates.

There is no more clear example of institutionalized misogyny, even today, than the Roman Catholic Church, which continues to

---

8. Wikipedia: Gender (Glover, D and Kaplan, C (2000) *Genders*, Routledge, New York, xxi).

cling to the expectation that healthy males, in a sufficient number to fill all the churches, will sign on to a life of celibate priesthood. The resulting sex abuse scandals are well documented, none more reeking of injustice than the abuse of nuns. Epitomizing the Church's hypocrisies, nuns impregnated through sexual abuse by male clergy have been forced to commit the added sin, in their minds, of abortion. For that matter, the fundamentalist arguments from all quarters on the question of abortion represent the quintessence of misogyny. Where is the rational justification in forcing a poor woman raped by her estranged husband to have her ninth child, whom she will be unable to feed?

One cannot consider the subject of misogyny without the ancient legend of Pygmalion coming to mind. Made famous by the Roman poet Ovid, the sculptor Pygmalion, disgusted with real women, sets about to sculpt a perfect one and then proceeds to fall in love with his marble creation. The romance ends happily when the goddess Aphrodite grants his wish to bring the statue to life. "But wait!" you cry, confused. "What relation can there be between this old love story and misogyny?"

As defined in *The Blackwell Dictionary of Sociology*,[9] misogyny as "a cultural attitude of hatred for females because they are female" (Johnson 2005, 197). Few men are unabashed in their hatred of women, and many who have steeped throughout their lives in this cultural attitude will vehemently deny having absorbed it. By no means, they will assert, do they harbor anything but fondness for a good-looking woman. That is emblematic of misogyny: along with the assumption of superiority, the nature of what he *loves* about women is solely physical. The attitude of disdain is so embedded and pervasive that few people of either gender can see the fine line that demarcates objectification from respect of personhood. The signals are especially confusing for young girls, who cannot be expected to appreciate the subtle distinction. To the ingenuous girl

---

9. Written by Allan G. Johnson, American sociologist who specialized in gender issues.

flattered by a charming rogue, the demeaning aspect of misogyny may be brought home only through subsequent abuse.

Thus Pygmalion: his presumptive right to pass judgment upon the whole female gender incorporates the axiom of male superiority. He turns to cold marble to mold his conception of the perfect female figure and falls in love with bloodless stone, a conditional love that requires as its object a well-formed, flawless body.

Based upon this tale, the play *Pygmalion*, written by George Bernard Shaw in 1912, further emphasizes its inherent misogyny. The well-known plot, adapted by the team of Lerner and Loewe in a musical version, *My Fair Lady*, involves a curmudgeonly bachelor, Professor Henry Higgins, who enters into a bet with his friend, Colonel Pickering, that he can turn a poor cockney flower seller, Eliza Doolittle, into a proper lady in six months. The gents are typically misogynistic, while the playwright was not. Shaw, who lived from 1856 until 1950, was an Irish firebrand, a polemicist in his contentious views, an insightful observer of human nature, and a superlative writer. The conclusion of his play does not adhere to the hackneyed denouement that would have Eliza marry the professor. She spurns him in the end.

To the playwright's horror, subsequent productions of the popular play took liberties with its unpopular conclusion. In testament to his true intentions, Shaw penned an essay, "What Happened Afterwards," that was added to later print editions. This essay may be seen online at bartleby.com. He explained with his inimitable mastery of wry satire why Eliza must reject marriage with Higgins. The happy ending, he writes, "is unbearable, not only because her little drama, if acted on such a thoughtless assumption, must be spoiled, but because the true sequel is patent to anyone with a sense of human nature in general, and of feminine instinct in particular" (paragraph 1). With his keen analytical sense and acerbic Irish wit, he concludes, "Galatea never does quite like Pygmalion: his relation to her is too godlike to be altogether agreeable" (paragraph 24).

Can we say, as Shaw implies, that Pygmalion was a misogynist? Shaw portrays Higgins as a man married to his mother, to whom no other woman could possibly measure up. Alan Jay Lerner, lyricist for the musical, captured the misogynist in the professor singing, "Why can't a woman be more like a man?" Shaw obviously admires the character of Eliza, drawing her with astute complexity, as he explains and defines, writing: "Eliza has no use for the foolish romantic tradition that all women love to be mastered, if not actually bullied and beaten....To admire a strong person and to live under that strong person's thumb are two different things" (paragraph 6). There can be slavish women and men alike. Shaw admits that, but he affirms that women are people, an admission at which a bona fide misogynist will balk.

In 1729, when Jonathan Swift wrote his straight-faced satire *A Modest Proposal*, the title of which goes on to read, "For preventing the children of poor people from being a burden to their parents or country, and for making them beneficial to the public," he used a rhetorical device related to irony known as apophysis or paralipsis. In the famous essay, published anonymously, he was mocking the heartless policies of Britain toward poverty, particularly the poor of Ireland, suggesting with satirical hyperbole that the Irish could sell their children as food. In other words, if they were so lacking in pity toward poor people, a resort to cannibalism would be a practical policy. The style has been taken up by many writers before and since to skewer outrageous irrationality by means of feigned agreement, but in the brutal, savage climate of these times, an age of radical Islam, acts of terrorism on crowds of innocents, assault weapons in the hands of lunatics and children, deliberate bombing of civilian populations, we dare not suggest cannibalism lest it be taken seriously. We must temporize. My *modest* proposal must be more so than Swift's.

It is a given that the human species has overpopulated the planet, its numbers growing exponentially, and that in the attempt to support this metastatic growth, it has polluted all critical resources. It should be obvious to any thoughtful and fair-minded person that since men have been in charge from time immemorial, they should be held responsible, and it is clear that by and large, they have no interest in rational means of controlling population growth. To the contrary, they are more likely to assert that every child conceived must be born and that each man must impregnate every female he fancies. While every child must be born, they do not all have to live. Since the male is patently superior and females are worthless, all the girls may be nipped in the bud, so to speak. Sons bring wealth and a secure old age.

Now for my modest proposal by which men may succeed in eliminating all females and at last, if unwittingly, curb the population in the process. Being so devilishly clever, they will have come up with a plan to avoid extinction by reproducing themselves in vitro, making it easy to weed out any conceptus with the incorrect chromosomes. With proper laboratory vessels in which to grow the embryo and gestate the fetus, the process of birth will be far more hygienic, uncomplicated, and agreeable than ever. Best of all, every child in the nursery will be male—forever after.

By the time female humans no longer exist, men will need to be able to clone themselves, or they must resort to parthenogenesis. As for sexual gratification, we might presume that after generations without it, libido will have become attenuated. Where it lingers, the condition will be treated with drugs to suppress testosterone. Robotics might have something to contribute on those lines—a sex object that turns on and off. There are always mannequins.

This masculine utopia is quickly materializing in some societies where it is acceptable to abort females or smother them at birth. To hasten the spread of this excellent refinement in humankind, older women must also be eliminated. This goal can be accomplished by denying them healthcare, easy enough with despots taking control over most of the world. A divine peace will come once women are extinct, the old having died and none born to replace them. No more will men be plagued by the crying, the screaming, and the senseless chatter. The distasteful female figure, so unseemly compared with the sleekness of the male, will no longer offend us with its bovine mammary glands and flabby derriere. The wretched, slavish, deficient creatures gone for good, men will create the perfect civilization, turning their superior minds to great intellectual, scientific, and artistic achievements and their bodies to feats of athleticism. Ample support for this prediction is there in human history: the ingenious discoveries and inventions of science and technology, all achieved by men; the monumental works of art and architecture, the magnificent musical masterpieces, all created by men. Compared to the dismal mediocrity of women, men are grand and noble beings. What have women produced besides babies? What more should they have?

Bizarre, unnatural, irrational, and an unjust phenomenon, the institutionalized hatred of women is one of the most extreme manifestations of the most extreme life-form on the planet. What are we to make of it? Misogyny is primeval, the legacy perhaps of the caveman. Women are weak, having on average less muscle mass than men. If she is weaker than myself, why should I not drag her by the hair into the cave? On this and so many other qualities, the male will feel justified in pronouncing women inferior. As for the great accomplishments of men, the Persian offered this:

> They say the lion and the lizard keep
> The court where Jamshyd gloried and drank deep,
> And Bahrám, that great hunter, the wild ass
> Stamps o'er his head, and he lies fast asleep! (Fitzgerald 1952, 49)

That nasty German, Nietzsche, said, "When you go to women, take your whip with you." My proposal is at once efficient and more modest.

COMMUNICATION

- *The Tower of Babel* -

The subject of communication, I daresay, has never been more urgent than in modern times when the internet is enabling and amplifying the crafty, cunning methods of propaganda. Brainwashing techniques, pernicious for their subtlety and sophistication, lie at the fingertips of any college marketing major, not to mention dictators or autocratic governments at work on a modern, cybernetic Tower of Babel built upon the destruction of trust. We are led to suspect all sources of information except those controlled by the Party, the Crown Prince, or the Supreme Leader. Everything else is "fake news" promulgated by "enemies of the people," while the current struggle against this ruinous state of affairs is disturbingly ineffectual. Communication is a broad topic deserving of thoughtful consideration, especially for the only species capable of speech.

In the first book of the Old Testament at Genesis 11:1-9, we find the folktale of the Tower of Babel, an origin myth explaining how mankind came to have different languages. The story goes that following the Flood, the people commenced building a high tower that would reach to heaven. In the interpretation of the Roman historian Josephus, God rebuked their arrogance by causing them to speak in diverse tongues so that they could no longer understand one another. "Thence did the Lord scatter them abroad upon the face of all the earth."

Other cultures have similar myths, and ancient historians tried to associate the biblical story with other accounts of early attempts at building a skyscraper, but the truth of the matter is otherwise. The human being is an inveterate explorer, a globetrotter, and as the species slowly spread around the world, groups became geographically isolated. As they remained thus sufficiently long enough to evolve the distinct physical traits we now call "race," they developed separate languages. As evidence that geography was determinative, areas close enough to allow interaction are linguistically related (the Romance or Asian languages as examples).

Language continues to evolve rapidly in modern times. In my own lifetime, seven plus decades, the *Merriam-Webster Collegiate Dictionary* has grown several inches thicker. Despite Winston Churchill's clever bon mot that Great Britain and America are two great nations "divided only by a common language," English has become the global lingua franca. Shallow thinkers offer the facile opinion that the dominance of the English language is the offshoot of American imperialism over recent centuries. The economic impact of American financial hegemony is a major factor, but I have concluded after long consideration that English prevails because it is most efficient, requiring fewer syllables in most instances. One can verify this point by counting syllables: "many thanks" versus "muchas gracias" or "merci beaucoup." Observe the labels on merchandise where different languages are required, and the case is even clearer: "Keep batteries away from children" becomes "Tenir les piles hors de la portée des enfants" and "Mantenga las pilas alejadas de los niños." *Quod erat demonstrandum.* The distinctive, rapid-fire staccato of Spanish-speaking people may be attributable to the fact that it takes them lots of syllables to express anything.

Important as spoken language was to the foundation of human society, and especially civilized society, the written word became equally if not more so, since oral traditions were circumscribed by the limits of human memory. Most languages evolved a phonetic alphabet, though Chinese was curiously late after stubborn adherence to a cumbersome ideographic style. Thanks to stone and chisel, papyrus, and graphite, a good deal of ancient knowledge and creativity has come down through history. Johannes Gutenberg, circa 1439, with his printing press, mechanized and simplified the dissemination of information. His printed Bible, Latin version, and Luther's German one the following century, enabled the Protestant Reformation. In an age of discovery and exploration, the technology quickly spread around the globe.

We must observe that there is a clear, unequivocal tension surrounding access to information, because knowledge is power. When every man can read and learn what is in the Bible, the Holy Roman Church and its infallible Pope lose their grip on him. If the Chinese peasantry were to master the thousands of ideographs representing their language, the dominion of the educated imperial class could end. Today, as a technology much more invasive than the printing press has globalized, the threat to power is acute, giving rise to desperate and sinister measures to control information. In many quarters, responsible journalism may result in mortal danger from a blood-thirsty potentate.

Stereotypically, the devil lures us in with wonders. The computer and its instant worldwide connection has changed our lives, brought fantastical possibilities, and become the indispensable means of managing a complex society with a population of unprecedented size. At the intersection of this technological advancement and population growth lies the publishing business, turned on its head as it becomes easier and cheaper for anyone to publish a book. Old-line houses long ago stopped publishing any book they did not solicit, while scores of small publishers filled the void for new writers or lesser lights. Targeting niche markets, these small presses may turn out a hundred titles a year from a thousand manuscripts reviewed, the favored genres being children's books and religious tracts.

With the invention of print-on-demand methods, self-publishing services sprang up and proliferated, so that any poor young person can now enter the Tower of Babel, dreaming of glory. In the last few years, the heated competition between such services has drawn the attention of the corporate world, with several imprints gathering under a corporate umbrella for advantage. Sales of the service—to writers, not readers—are relegated to Asian call centers, where those who can speak any Pidgin English are taught a high-pressure, misleading sales pitch. Pity the naive youngster so persuaded to whom the best advice is to keep his day job. The truth is that there are now more writers than readers, just as Samuel Johnson remarked regarding the invention of the printing press. Nevertheless, the self-publishing phenomenon is tailor-made for the older generation, those like myself who seek only to leave, if available only in the clouds, their thoughts, their history, and their passions.

The internet has made cacophony of human discourse, and we must wonder what genius is being lost in the uproarious bedlam. For all the increased potential in communication, there is a blindness to it, a groping in cyberspace, the reaches of which are no less than outer space. Attesting to the enormous scope of this phenomenon is its concomitant search engine, the so-called "browser," yielding at a click the cornucopia of all that is material or subliminal in the world. What needle is being overlooked in the haystack of information—a cure for cancer, the key to harnessing atomic fusion, or solutions to overpopulation and world hunger? The problem is finding that needle and sifting the wheat from the chaff. In times past, the filters were a matter of class; the aristocracy received the education and became the intelligentsia. In the twentieth century, a kind of meritocracy emerged with college boards assessing the capability of applicants, government research grants being awarded on merit, and unsolicited manuscripts being accepted for review by major publishers. The online culture is undermining all that. Anything and everything can be bought online. A college degree? Click here. Publish your novel? Click there. If you have the cure for cancer, you could post it on your Facebook page or your blog. Google would find it on page 210, 331, 865,000…………..

Beside the needle in a haystack, another metaphor is applicable here: the old English admonishment against hiding one's light under a bushel. The proverb alludes to a passage in the New Testament, Matthew 5:15-16 (King James Version), in which Jesus says, "Neither do men light a candle and put it under a bushel…Let your light so shine before men that they may see your good works." This proverb enlists us to use whatever opportunities we have to do good for our fellow man, humbly and without thought of praise. Whether in following the Gospel or for one's personal satisfaction, the free pursuit of our individual passions—for science or the arts—might light the world. In the Tower of Babel that civilized society has become, these candles are destined for obscurity under a bushel, however hard we might try to let them shine.

Nonetheless, we are connected by technology in the instant manner of neurons, cells in the nervous system of a social organism. With the advent of the smartphone, everyone we know—from close friends and relatives to casual acquaintances—becomes a tap and a swipe away. The young are so accustomed to this way of communicating that they elude face-to-face contact and even vocal interchange. We still have to talk to one another, though that can be a complex process, the purview of which is linguistics, the science of language.

The author who has done more than anyone perhaps in highlighting that science is Deborah Tannen, linguistics professor at Georgetown University. She studies and writes about the psychological nuances of our conversational styles and especially the damage caused by misunderstanding each other. Her book, *That's Not What I Meant,* is subtitled *How Conversational Style Makes or Breaks Relationships.* In other books, she has explored the dissonant styles of men versus women and parents versus children, uncovering as well the sources of sibling rivalry and angry grudge matches. An important linguistic concept she has popularized is that of the metamessage, discussed in the essay "Marriage and Children."

The metamessage, a subliminal meaning that is not expressly conveyed in words, took on a personal relevance with respect to my sister whose mother-in-law was the virtuoso of this verbal subterfuge. The avoidance of eye contact, the thrumming of her fingers on her chest, the coy giggle when she feigned a Freudian slip—these were only the observable signals by which she controlled her only son. The poor man would writhe in angry but hopeless resistance to her power, while she could appear innocent to perplexed onlookers. By the time he was relieved by the death of this harpy, he was nearly seventy-five.

Even a cursory reading of Dr. Tannen's work impresses upon us the complexity of the subject and the immeasurable potential for misunderstanding in our every conversation. An avoidance of such miscues in our relationships requires a special sensitivity to distinctions in conversational style and the subtle signals by which these styles are expressed. Too often people leap to unwarranted conclusions about emotional content and end in needless quarrels. Should we wonder why young people avoid eye contact, let alone speech?

More far reaching than linguistics in the study of communication is semiotics, the study of signs, an arcane field referred to as the "philosophy of language." Since communication between humans goes much deeper than words, we can imagine a broad scope for this philosophy from graffiti to the meaning of dreams. There is body language, sign language, semaphore, dance, art, icons, logos, and on and on. Music is a prime example; to quote author Richard Middleton, a music professor at Newcastle University in the United Kingdom, "There are strong arguments that music occupies a semiological realm which…has developmental priority over verbal language" (Middleton 1990, 172). Before they can talk, infants respond to music; some believe they do so in the womb.

Here too in the musical realm is the perfect Tower of Babel in which, as I made clear in my essay on modernism, we have lost the ability to communicate. Uniquely, music is the language of the emotions, and thus we should expect it to be universally understood. There is emotional significance even in the music of differing cultures, but when the composition of music is upended at random for the sheer mischief of novelty, audiences abandon it. Ironically, the failure of music professionals themselves to appreciate its essence as language has eroded our understanding and appreciation of music. One may argue that popular music in all its myriad branches—rock, rap, hip hop, and so on ad nauseam—still conveys emotional meaning to the masses. My rejoinder is indisputable: A careful listen reveals extreme limitations in the sound and the scope of its message. The sound is nearly uniform, consisting of a high decibel throbbing and often no more than three separate tones, while the substance is an unvaried theme of rapacious lust and depravity. The proof that even this base level of the medium fails to communicate is that it is not readily reproducible, not in the way that popular songs, heretofore, might be remembered and sung.

Some might claim that all human emotion boils down to mating except for the evidence of classical masterpieces: the enormous intellectual achievement of Baroque polyphony, the union of music and dance in classical ballet and of music with drama in opera, particularly that of the incomparable Italians; the religious music of the great cathedrals stirs the deepest spirituality. Because modern times have produced no counterparts, this form of musical communication may likely fade and slowly die.

Among the more vexing absurdities of contemporary communication is that the more numerous the means, the less we are able to communicate. The invention of the telephone was hailed as miraculous, the last word, faster than a telegram or letter, eliminating the quaint practice of presenting one's calling card to the butler in hope of finding someone at home. Why would anyone need a faster means of communicating than the telephone? Why indeed. A good deal of infrastructure was needed before it became practical. Transmission lines were stretched between poles that marched across the landscape, marring its pristine beauty in the opinion of many. The lines joined to homes and other buildings, and cords led to the telephones themselves. One might view this system as a kind of web analogous to the digital technology that later evolved.

Along the way, the dependence on lines and wires must have begun to seem unduly restrictive. In 1973, almost a century after Bell's patent, Motorola demonstrated the first mobile or cell phone. This clever device required new infrastructure—those ugly cell towers—yet it caught on quickly. In the way that progress accelerates as science builds upon discovery and invention, the computer age dawned with its incredible capabilities. People with these wonderful machines were enabled to write to one another via email: no stationery, no stamp, and no postal service needed. Invisible signals bounced from global satellites to create a new web, the internet. No sooner had email spread in popularity than new "smart" phones became small brain cells, handheld computers with access to the web.

Communication is now instantaneous—potentially—but there's the rub. The myriad ways for us to contact one another do not make it easier. The old telephone, which must be called the landline to distinguish it from its freewheeling successor, is disappearing but for the few remaining in the hands of old fogeys who refuse to change their ways, and those few phones are never answered, because they have become monopolized by solicitors and con artists. Not to worry! Everyone now is assumed to have a smartphone, even some old fogeys. With a smartphone, one may send email without sitting in front of his desktop computer, but one may also send a text message, the method preferred of the younger generation. One might even call and talk or preferably leave a voicemail message—heaven forbid we should encounter a real person, trapping us into the tedious hassle of spontaneous speech.

If we count a posted letter, which depends on a gravely dysfunctional and shrunken quasi-government agency, there are at least five or six possible ways to get in touch. This is the description of a

Tower of Babel: When we must convey information, we must choose among several options that may or may not bring our message to the attention of its intended recipient. Punished for our arrogance, like the ancient people of legend, we may as well be speaking different languages.

It cannot be denied that there is a good deal of information easily available and of great benefit to us, but ironically, too much information has brought about an odd state of gathering and festering doubt. Reality is always a shifting concept. Even scientific certainties fall to the progress of knowledge, and conclusions based on statistics are often incorrectly understood or manipulated to support a theory or bias. Nefarious actors, worms in the apple of so-called social media, deliberately use the new means of communication to sow mistrust, propagate an ideology, or pit tribe against tribe for personal gain or power. How can the rest of us hope to sort the true from the false?

The Tower of Babel that I have described is a threat to human communication in modern times. Social stability relies on consensus in regard to authority, on a general agreement as to which person or institution is competent to have the last word on critical topics. We may doubt or disagree, but the majority must be prepared to trust. When that trust has been undermined in large segments of the population, chaos will reign. The liberal democracies of the West, given their freedom of speech and of the press, are particularly vulnerable to hostile actors. People will come to believe only what they want to believe, so that whatever reality is coming to fruition—the rising of the seas, increasing inefficacy of antibiotics, or mounting starvation in overpopulated regions—will ensure calamity.

Trust must become our top priority, the first thing we safeguard by the strict censure of fakery and slander. I fear that the dissolution of trust, along with the degradation of our ability to communicate effectively, will catapult us inexorably from the Book of Genesis to the Book of Revelation. Revisiting that apocalyptic hallucination is sobering in its many modern parallels: the earth destroyed by fire, earthquakes, smoke blackening the sun, and wormwood poisoning rivers and springs. This prophecy is getting too close for comfort. That distant rumbling: is it thunder we hear or the approach of the Four Horsemen?

TRAVEL

- You Can't Get There from Here -

As I sit at Manchester airport awaiting my return flight to the States, the place bustles with fellow travelers, domestic and international, going their separate ways on their separate missions, and I ponder the peculiar inclination on the part of humankind toward wanderlust, thanks to which the species has populated the globe. In modern times, travel is more common than ever. It is obligatory. Anyone who does not participate is so anomalous as to be outcast. This is the case even as the experience grows increasingly unpleasant.

Long ago, to go to Grandmother's house required a horse to pull a sleigh "over the river and through the woods." At the time, horse-drawn carriages, along with sailing ships, were the only means of travel. The steam engine and internal combustion engine that followed on its heels changed all that abruptly. Today it is hard to impress upon people the vital role horses played for many centuries.

I am not old enough to remember horses pulling hansom cabs through city streets, but I remember when travel of any greater distance was done on a train. By modern standards, trains were slow but luxurious and comfortable. Dining cars had linen table cloths and napkins, and the rail line would serve on its emblematic china. There were smoking cars and observation cars, and on a long trip, one could bunk at night in a Pullman car.

There was a keen sense of romance to trains: the anticipation of the journey, the excitement rising as the destination neared, the views rolling past, and an ever-changing tableau. Even for those looking on, watching it pass or hearing its distant, lonely whistle, the train was evocative. As children, I and my chums walked on the tracks, skipping over the ties or balancing on the rails that converged on some distant vanishing point. The tracks were lined with wild flowers, changing varieties each season—blue gentian, yellow daisies, and Queen Anne's lace.

A journey by train was terribly exciting for a child, going to new places and seeing all the sights along the way as the train sped past. I still have a vivid memory of the perilous walk between cars where a person could look down and see the tracks fly by underneath. The passage was closed but unheated and had a particular smell, something like damp straw. The scenery from the train was beautiful regardless of the season as the train passed through flat farmland dotted with far-flung houses and barns, cattle herds grazing, or horses gamboling. On some trips, mountains gradually rose in the distance, at times topped with snow that glistened gold at sunset. To be served dinner in the dining car seemed a sinful luxury, as did the fresh sheets in the sleeping compartment where the steady rhythm of the rails, the clickety-clack of the wheels, was sedative.

Around the middle of the last century, the ages-old dream of our species to fly became a reality with the inauguration of passenger airlines. With those first propeller planes, a train trip of days was reduced to hours, but air flight was expensive, the exclusive province of the wealthy. Seats were roomy and comfortable, meals were served in-flight, and alcohol flowed. Stewardesses wore smart uniforms, the fashion model figure being a qualification for the job. Compared with railways, even greater romance and excitement was associated with flying. At that time, it was a unique experience to be taken above the clouds, watching the earth, the houses, and the rivers and bays shrink with distance. The commanding view of cities and towns from aloft or of the countryside—a bucolic tapestry—felt like a miracle. As a teen, I sometimes drove with friends to the airport just to sit in the lounge and watch the planes through the lofty plate glass windows as they landed or took off, expecting every minute to catch a glimpse of a celebrity among the well-dressed passengers hurrying past. Yes, one dressed up to fly on a plane!

In no time, it seemed, jet engines replaced propellers, and the world again became a smaller place. Grandmother could live across the sea and still expect you to come for Christmas, because now you could *fly* over the river—and over the wood—provided you could afford it. Flying was still an expensive proposition, and the people able to hop on a plane at will were dubbed "jet-setters." How did this class come to be such a large portion of the population?

It is a one-word answer: deregulation. In the United States, President Carter signed the bill deregulating airlines in 1978. The aim was to create competition among airlines that would make travel more affordable. The first result put some carriers out of business. Surviving ones merged, a process that continues to this day. Fares did go down before creeping up again. In retrospect, there can be no doubt that the glory days of luxury and comfort in commercial aviation were over, and the ensuing era brought the evils we witness today. Most curious, and still a mystery to me, was the collaboration of airlines with credit card companies, seemingly enabling any person with credit to fly virtually for free. This collusion has filled the skies with a swarm of planes and airports with mobs of people. It is the reason that anyone who yearns to see this world before seeing the next can hop on a plane and do so on the magic carpet of his credit card. People now fly at the drop of a hat. A destination wedding in the South Pacific? I'll be there! An African safari? Sign me up! Expedition to Antarctica? Why not! They travel, they send their children and then their grandchildren, lest the young ones fail to become men and women of the world.

From my perspective, having known this world as it once was, this utopian dream in the developed nations has become a nightmare. The prevalence of air travel soon made planes a favorite target for terrorism, leading to security protocols that grew irrational and contrived. Lest we be accused of "profiling" the terrorist, we must be sure to push Granny in her wheelchair through the x-ray. Even more degrading than airline security are the flight delays and cancellations. Unlike those evil days of government regulation, there is now no certainty that an airline ticket will get you to a certain place at a certain time. When there were but a few air carriers, there were planes to spare. If one was grounded for a mechanical problem, another was readily available, whereas today, anxious passengers ready to board are told they must wait for another plane that is on its way from a distant city.

With the skies clogged with aircraft and the airports with people, frequent disturbances are inevitable. A storm anywhere on the continent sends ripples far and wide, upsetting the whole interconnected system for days to come, while would-be travelers camp out in the airport, sprawled across seats or on a filthy floor with a backpack for a pillow. Nearby hotels fill up immediately. Under the circumstances, it should be incumbent upon the airports to provide tents and sleeping bags or at least to rent them. Young people do not seem to consider such deprivations sufficiently inconvenient to be a deterrent. Savvy with the smartphone, they can finagle a seat on the next plane out to Timbuktu and double back from there to their original destination.

Depending on the length of the journey, the equation favoring air flight for its speed is changed, with travelers coming to realize they might as well drive. But highway systems are equally problematic: roads under construction after years of neglect, occluded by overwhelming traffic and washed out by floods or other climate disasters. At times and in places, it appears we are returning to the days of the horse and carriage that easily bogged down on muddy, unpaved roads, but the problem is growing numbers of cars. The fact is inescapable despite wishful thinkers who consider it arguable. Idealists believe that the solution to traffic congestion is to refrain from building roads. Without roads, they assert, people will neither buy cars nor drive; old people will walk however far to the doctor's office or wait in the rain in their wheelchairs for a bus or two. Commuters without access to trains will get to work by rowboat, or swim across the river if necessary, and walk from there, arriving at the office with pneumonia.

Like planes and trains, automobiles were once an agreeable means of travel. A superhighway had two lanes in either direction, and one was for passing, which a driver might accomplish without worrying about a collision with cars in the multiple lanes of today's superhighway. A road trip was the ultimate freedom. One could drive for as long as one wanted, stopping along the way to rest and refuel. At dusk on a long journey, the road would come upon a small town with a motel or two of which at least one would have the neon "Vacancy" sign lit. In the morning, if the accommodation did not have a cafe, one might find breakfast in the town. Outside an inn or coffee shop, a sign pointing its arrow to the words "Eat Here!" would be blinking. Inside would be a short-order cook serving the locals and local color. Even on the turnpikes, there were decent places to stop until the fast-food franchises took over.

For all the debasement I have described, most people will insist that they love to travel, and adding to the irony, the majority of these are old retired people who worked and saved with the dream of traveling. These same people, having extolled the joys of gallivanting, will go on to expound in great detail the most hair-raising disasters endured on those trips, tours, or treks: flights cancelled, connections missed, sleepless nights at the airport, or river cruises spent on the tour bus when rivers were too low to float a boat.

Cruises are popular in general, whether on river boats or enormous ships that amount to floating cities. Not being a seafaring person, I have no experience of cruising. I contend that ships are picturesque only as seen from the shore. I find it hard to imagine being on one for an extended time, force-fed meal after meal, day after day, bored silly on a deck chair baking in the sun, enduring, as Sherlock Holmes put it, "the insufferable fatigues of idleness."

There was a time in my younger days when I yearned to see other parts of the world: Hawaii, for example, and the Canadian Rockies. I was too busy, I thought; there would be time enough later in my declining years after I retired. As considerable time went by, what little travel I managed became fraught, uncertain, and unpleasant, and what declined more than my physical ability was any desire to participate in the aggravating, deplorable experience. It is hard to say what now sets me apart from the legions of people signing up for their indispensable adventures, but I have a few theories.

I differ from younger people in remembering a time when travel was slower, easier, and more comfortable. Without this basis for comparison, they are oblivious. To pull on their clodhoppers, stuff a backpack, and Uber over to the airport, there hoping to board a plane going anywhere sometime within the next several days, appears to them the epitome of pleasure. Being young with plenty of energy and seeing no greater use for it, they want for nothing more than escape. As I have observed, the older generation, those who should know better, are equally willing to endure wretched, distressing conditions in order to touch the ground of the places on their bucket list. They *must* see the Taj Mahal before they die—from the back of an Indian elephant!

Maybe I have slowly gotten old and, in the process, more rigid, or perhaps I have never been flexible enough to appreciate the joys of travel despite its occasional inconvenience. I enjoy my dependable routine, the creature comforts, regular meals, and a five-star hotel over a hostel any day, and I would be loath to voluntarily sacrifice amenities. These are factors, but there is lately another aspect to my resistance, and as it must seem like a rationalization, I hope readers will grant me the benefit of the doubt.

Since my childhood, I have had a keen sense of identity with sentient beings—not only family pets but wild creatures as well. A bird perched in a tree would stir an awareness of bony claws gripping the branch as though I had once been a bird. In a former life? I wondered. I staked out the wooded area on our land with my binoculars, hoping to glimpse some rara avis, a migrant brambling or black redstart. I have sighted those two birds as an adult, but at the time, my knowledge of their natural history was nil. I did not realize how unlikely such a sighting would have been from where I sat. I made friends with squirrels, feeding them peanuts and even patiently coaxing one to eat from my hand. That particular fellow was honored with the name J. Alfred Prufrock, compliments of T. S. Eliot's "The Love Song of J. Alfred Prufrock." My fondest dream was to live in a cabin in the woods with the woodland creatures as my friends: the birds, squirrels, and deer.

With my subsequent interest in Buddhism and the practice of meditation, this innate feeling of identity has blossomed. As explained in my essay on the subject, a principle goal of meditation is to observe the workings of the mind: its thought processes, its essence absent thought, clear and alert, the fundamental nature of sensation and perception, and slowly by inference to uncover the reality of what we call *self*. Through this practice, we come to know over time the conditional nature of this earthly life. All we perceive, all we are, is karmic, the effect of cause, yet also rising to the surface in the meditative state is the intuition of a deeper, ultimate reality of something transcendent that we must call *oneness*. The true experience of oneness is the realization of the self as singular identity.

My reading led me to understand the principle, but the experience itself is wordless, inexplicable. Suddenly *I am* the whole universe and filled with a serene assurance that I cannot be separated from it. I need not be conscious of these things, being identical with them. It is but a small step to extrapolate that the myriad wonders of this world that travelers are so desperate to see *with their own eyes* I have no need to see, having seen them with my inner eye. I have no need to set eyes on the Taj Mahal, Mount Temple from Lake Louise in Alberta, Canada, or the rainbows and waterfalls on the rainy island of Maui. An enormous benefit accrues in saving me untold aggravation and discomfort, not to mention loads of money!

When friends and family members chide me about my reluctance to subject myself to the rigors of modern travel, asserting most ardently its compensatory joys, I am wont to remind them of the Belle of Amherst, Emily Dickinson, who never ventured far from the family manse in Amherst, Massachusetts, where her grandfather, Samuel, was among the founders of Amherst College. Without exposure to the world at large, her amazing intellect allowed her a meaningful life, which she reflected in her poetry to the benefit of readers for generations. She was a famous recluse and a compulsive poetess, leaving more than a thousand poems discovered after her death by her younger sister. Amid this wealth, which in some respect reads like the cryptic diary of a heretic, she wrote, "I never saw a moor, I never saw the sea; Yet know I how the heather looks, And what a wave must be…" (Dickinson 2016, 48).

The Buddha himself, having rejected asceticism, sat under the tree of wisdom for six years, and only upon attaining enlightenment set forth to teach his Middle Way to liberation. A millennium later, his heir, Bodhidharma, brought the teaching to China with some initial difficulty. Legend has it that upon arriving, he was met by a pompous mogul who asked him to epitomize the Buddhist message. Bodhidharma replied with a question, "Who are you?" Missing the existential point of this response, the potentate became incensed at not being recognized by the stranger. Bodhidharma retreated in disgust to a mountain monastery and meditated facing a wall for nine years, becoming known as "the wall-sitting monk."

He had *traveled* to China. More centuries later, Dogen Zenji of Japan also traveled to China, bringing the same teaching back upon his return. Suzuki Roshi brought Zen from Japan to San Francisco in the twentieth century. For these masterful teachers, travel had a definite purpose, a mission apart from seeing the sights. Today, the mission of ubiquitous travel can be anything from a visit to Grandmother's house to attending a sporting event or an expedition around Cape Horn by chance to see a penguin.

Though I live mainly in the States, I am responsible for family property in England and thus am forced to commute back and forth on occasion. So here I sit at Manchester airport waiting to board my flight, which has been delayed, and wondering what is wrong with me that I do not relish the experience of uncertainty as much as those, young and old, sitting around me. Some get up to get more coffee or use the restroom. Others loosen their jackets and try to get comfortable, take out a book, or plug in their mobile device to charge the battery. The usual routine is for the delay to start at one hour, followed by another after apologies, and so on until passengers become irate. Only then is any explanation given, or I should say excuse. They might as well say, "You can't get there from here."

In this state, I conveyed the situation to my American friend, Anna, in a text, receiving in her reply the suggestion that I write this essay and add it to the collection. No, I did not write the whole thing at the airport but had nearly completed it by the time the plane touched down. Now having missed the connecting flight home, there is plenty of time to see it done. Oh, the joys!

JUST CALL ME ALICE

- Through the Looking Glass -

Whenever something in the world seems upside down, expectations inverted, my friend Anna, who contributes to my weekly blog, likes to say, "Just call me Alice!" As we are both septuagenarians, these occasions arise frequently due to the accumulating discrepancies between life as we once knew it and as it now is. Contrary to the cliché that history repeats itself, it never does so with any exactness. At some point, we must consider that we have lived too long; we have gone through the looking glass.

Take, for example, negative interest rates. I may not be sophisticated as to matters of finance, but neither am I unfamiliar with that sphere or naive about it. I learned and have always claimed that money comes to money. If you save money, you will be able to lend it out at a certain interest rate, and it will grow. Over a lifetime, a prudent person could save enough to retire and live, if modestly, on the interest. Should interest rates sink to zero, one would face the dreaded necessity of spending the principal, praying the while not to outlive it. The idea that a rate of interest might be less than zero—in the negative territory—belongs on the other side of the looking glass, forcing me to join Anna in the refrain, "Just call me Alice!" What can it conceivably mean? Would a depositor be required to pay the bank for storing his accounts? Would lenders become uncommonly charitable, giving away money with the expectation of only partial repayment? Curiouser and curiouser! Modern society has become strange, but first let us consider what

Alice found when she dozed on a snowy day by the fire playing chess with her kitten—according to Lewis Carroll, that is.

As the glass over the mantle turns to mist, allowing Alice's trespass, she speculates with the kitten that looking glass milk is not good to drink. She notices that the reflection of printed words is backward, and thus YKCOWREBBAJ. Going deeper into looking glass world, she discovers the garden of talking flowers where the rose is queen and common flies are fantastical hybrids: the Rocking-Horse-Fly, the Bread-and-Butterfly, and the Snap-Dragonfly. When she tries to return to the house, she learns that to arrive anywhere, one must go in the opposite direction. She moves deeper, encountering characters from nursery rhymes like the twins Tweedle Dum and Tweedle Dee, who recite the inimitable verse "The Walrus and the Carpenter," in which the sun shines with all its might in the middle of the night. She puzzles over the reasoning of these two, as stated by Tweedle Dee: "If it was so, it might be; if it were so, it would be; but as it isn't, it ain't. That's logic!" (Carroll 1999, 32)

Alice soon realizes that looking glass world is a chessboard and the warring sides are the White and the Red monarchs, she herself being a White pawn. Guided by the Red Queen across the chessboard, she passes through the "wood where things have no names" (Carroll 1999, 28), forgetting her own name until leaving it. She meets the White Queen, who confounds her with the rule of living backwards: "Jam tomorrow and jam yesterday, but never jam today," because there is jam only "every *other* day" (Carroll 1999, 44). Another example of living backwards, explains the Queen, is the King's messenger, in prison in advance of his trial. The commitment of the crime comes last.

In the next chapter, she comes across another creature from a nursery rhyme, Humpty Dumpty, sitting precariously on a narrow wall, who explains why it makes more sense to celebrate unbirthdays. He does the math: 365 days a year minus one birthday leaves 364 *unbirthdays*. Obviously much preferable! Before they end their "unsatisfactory" conversation, he defines the neologisms in the first lines of "Jabberwocky":

> Twas brillig and the slithy toes
> Did gyre and gimbal in the wabes,
> All mimsy were the borogoves
> And the mome raths outgrabe. (Carroll 1999, 58)

Did you know that a *borogove* "is a thin, shabby looking bird with its feathers sticking out all round"? I didn't either. In the end, Humpty Dumpty falls off the wall, and the White King is obliged to summon all his horses and men, as promised, to put him back together—if possible! The King asks Alice if she sees his messengers on the road, and she replies, "I see nobody on the road." Demonstrating that in this mirror image universe words are to be taken literally, the King remarks, "I wish I had such eyes to be able to see Nobody!"

She reaches the far side of the chessboard, after being saved from the Red Knight by the White Knight, and is crowned a queen herself. The ensuing wild party devolves into chaos, and Alice seizes the Red Queen, shaking her. She awakes back where she belongs, shaking her kitten.

The "Alice" books are the height of silliness, befitting only children. Here on the correct side of the looking glass, which adults are expected to inhabit, are no nonsensical, fantastical dreams, just hard reality. We can laugh at the strange adventures of Alice without any danger of losing our way down a rabbit hole or through a mirror, but watch out! The real world can be just as rife with silly nonsense. Milk that is not good to drink? Now we have milk made of soy, almonds, or oats. Have you tasted it? Mirror image letters? Look in your rearview mirror when you hear a siren, and you will see ECNALUBMA inverted to AMBULANCE. Talking flowers? Do we not "say it with flowers"? As for hybrid insects, the real world has only their constituent parts: no Bread-and-Butterflies, simply bread, butter, and butterflies; no Snap-Dragonflies, just snapdragons and dragonflies; no Rocking-Horse-Flies, only rocking horses and horseflies. However, I find two insects that could well come from the looking glass world: the camel cricket, resembling the camel but able to leap several feet straight into the air, and the earwig, tiny denizen of damp places with a scorpion's tail. Easiest of all to find in the real world is the "wood where things have no names." Anyone of a certain age wanders into it several times a day. Just call me Alice!

I was hard pressed to find further parallels, because nonsense is hard to remember. Giving the mind no way to relate to it, it slips the grip like an eel, which is how the White King described his Anglo-Saxon messenger who skipped up and down and "wriggled like an eel." However, as I thought about going in a direction opposite your destination in order to arrive there, I was put in mind of a light show I pass often at Christmastime, a spectacular display that one pays to drive through. I can see a good deal of it from the highway—and I'm especially fond of the flying reindeer—but could never determine how one would enter it. Consulting a map, I found that one has to leave the highway going away from the show and double back on a small road that crosses the highway and enters the park. I should have known, Alice!

After the Red Queen runs at top speed across the chessboard, dragging Alice along, she explains why they have not gotten anywhere. "Here, you see, it takes all the running you can do to keep in the same place" (Carroll 1999, 20). Is that not the experience of the modern shopping mall? The White Queen's description of living backwards seems only natural for a life gone through the looking glass. Of many equivalents today, there is the credit card economy—spending money before one earns it, buying things one neither needs nor has the room for.

Illogical, nonsensical use of language, vaudevillian puns, are comedy material, but we stumble upon them in daily life. Ordering groceries online, I discovered under each item a box checked for "substitute this item." To me, this should mean "substitute this item for something else that is out of stock." By trial and error, I learned that leaving the checkmark means "*provide* a substitute if this item is out of stock." If the shopper will not accept a substitute for that item, he must uncheck the box. Likewise, in an online gift registry, next to the item I wanted to give, I saw "0 of 1 purchased." Did that mean one had been requested by the registrants and it had been purchased, leaving none available? I learned it meant one had been requested and none had yet been purchased, in other words "0 purchased of 1." I gave a gift certificate instead!

Enough of childish nonsense. These days we all know from our "news feeds," a term once used only in relation to The Associated Press, how awash we are in more serious matters that defy logic and add to the impression of a world turned inside out. In many authoritarian regimes, citizens take to the streets in a pitiable attempt to overthrow a dictator: Russia, Syria, Venezuela, Burma, and the once-free city of Hong Kong. On the other hand, in the most famous democracy in history, a minority of the electorate takes up arms to *install* their dictator. In that same strange nation, the United States, where white police seem to make a practice of killing black civilians and one would expect the black civilians to retaliate, we see white civilians kill white police. Just call me Alice!

The political arena is a veritable wellspring of irrationality. Not long ago a political aspirant would snuff out his career through the sin of "flip-flopping," as it was called: making a promise or swearing fidelity to an idea and later backpedaling. Such a person would be lost to the other side of the looking glass. Today, it is common practice for the party in power to meet with dogged resistance from opponents to any paltry amount of government spending, only to have those same opponents bankrupt the treasury as soon they recapture control. No one blinks an eye; voters are jaded. So much for the cardinal sin of flip-flopping. For all the world, there must be a turnstile on the looking glass!

As civilization frays about the edges and society fragments into tribes, the one concern becomes power, leading to the most outrageous examples of hypocrisy. A populist leader may stroke his followers with the cadence of a preacher, and they will swear allegiance as to a tribal chieftain, one whose obvious superiority confers absolute, unquestionable power. Even if their tribe is a tiny portion of the nation, they will cling to a firm belief that they are the true patriots, upholders of democracy. Only their votes should be counted. As they break laws, they crow in consummate sincerity about defending the rule of law.

The culture is no less fruitful a source of ironical dissonance. Less than a century ago, it was a terrible disgrace to become pregnant out of wedlock. At the very least, the woman and her child faced a most uncertain future. They might be social outcasts unless her father stood with his shotgun—literally or figuratively—at their hasty wedding ceremony. The predicament gave birth, so to speak, to many a torrid Victorian novel until the advent of our modern, more reliable methods of birth control—and as the White Queen would say, living backward. Now the first thing the young couple wants to do is to practice living together, as though however long in the same apartment will tally with a lifelong troth. If they are still in love, they will have a child, by which time, and only then, it will begin to seem prudent for them to marry. The widespread acceptance of this inversion perpetuates the suspicion of the pregnant bride. Did she connive to ensnare the unwitting groom, omit her birth control, and feign pregnancy?

In days of old, as I like to say, indeed not more than fifty years ago, grown women wore dresses around the house, to work, to church, and at all social occasions. They might at times choose to wear slacks, but they seemed comfortable in dresses and skirts at any time. Their daughters likewise were attired in dresses. Some fifty years ago, they all slipped through the looking glass, coming to consider that by no means were they comfy in those dresses. They declared they were far more at ease stuffing themselves into tight-fitting denim. Had they all been mesmerized, collectively, by Levi Strauss & Company? The most puzzling aspect of the business is that these same young, modern women, in their denim uniforms, now are choosing to put their little daughters in dresses—frilly, feminine, fanciful dresses. We must surmise that these poor little girls, yearning to come of age, will beg to be allowed their first pair of jeans! Clothing styles may change fundamentally over time, and I confess to a tendency to harp on the outrage, particularly the immutable popularity of jeans.

These days, I am far more disturbed by a phenomenon that appears to represent considerable leakage through the looking glass. Despite a great accumulation of knowledge widespread in the population, there is a frightful dearth of common sense. Specific instances of this problem are difficult to collect, since they slither away from the mind like eels or the Anglo-Saxon messenger of the White King. Often they involve distinct aspects of a job or profession with which only a person in that position would be familiar. Many such arise in the medical profession, for example, where in recent times holders of the purse strings have labored hard to reduce the delivery of patient care to algorithms, thereby cutting out the cost of highly trained physicians and forcing the experienced ones into early retirement. The patient's fifteen-minute appointment is spent with his doctor at a laptop or tablet, clicking boxes on a template in order to boost the fee.

At each annual physical exam, the doctor is required to give the same patient the same advice—that he or she should quit smoking, lose weight, and get more exercise. Common sense should tell anyone that the patient already knows what he should do, but the physician must check off these boxes in order to be paid, while he and the patient shake their heads and roll their eyes as if to say "Just call me Alice!"

Initially, the move to digitalize the doctor's office seemed a good idea. Computer software would allow doctors to type their patient notes so that records would be more legible and efficient to store, but the creators of this software had more visionary schemes in mind. These Einsteins would condense the whole of medical knowledge into specialized computer programs, allowing the "healthcare provider" to enter a person's symptoms and retrieve from his genius computer the diagnosis and recommended treatment. An email to the local chemist for the requisite pill, and the fifteen-minute appointment was done. Nowhere in evidence, since this revolution took hold, has common sense been exercised. It would have informed the computer nerds what every practicing physician knows, at least on the doctor's side of the looking glass. Each case presents some unique aspect and challenge. Patients and their maladies cannot be expected to leap from the medical textbooks, let alone high-tech machines.

The coronavirus pandemic that swept the world beginning in 2019 occasioned some egregious and blatant examples of folly, first among which was the mask business. Common sense should tell us that if a highly infectious and deadly respiratory virus is spreading that kills a person's lung cells, we would be advised to keep the microbes out of our lungs by any means possible. The majority of us, having long ago accepted the existence of organisms invisible to the naked eye, thanks to the invention of the microscope, adopted the practice of wearing a facial covering when around other people. Some more cantankerous and churlish individuals viewed the whole idea as silly, exaggerated, an infringement of their civil rights. Others have been intelligent, educated professionals benighted as to the meaning of "exponential," as in the way a mutated cell may start to divide *exponentially* and grow into a malignant tumor, exactly the way an infectious disease can spread rapidly from one case to millions. Even educated people may follow Alice through the looking glass.

Look up "common sense" on Google or Wikipedia, and the first result retrieved is the Thomas Paine pamphlet of 1776 that fired up the American colonials at the start of the revolution against Britain. Entitled "Common Sense," the pamphlet is still in print and remains the all-time best-selling American publication. Paine argued passionately against the rule of monarchs and aristocrats, asserting that self-rule by the common man made *common sense* and that America had the chance to set an example by extricating itself from the immoral power of kings and lords. He relied repeatedly on his title "Common Sense":

> Some, perhaps, will say that after we have made it up with Britain, she will protect us…common sense will tell us that the power which has endeavored to subdue us is of all others the most improper to defend us. Conquest may be effected under the pretext of friendship…and ourselves be, at last, cheated into slavery. (Paine 2016, 54)

In this historical context, America, trapped on the chessboard of kings, queens, knights, bishops, and pawns, fought its way out of the looking glass world.

All the ancient religions, which by definition depend on the preservation of tradition and lore worthy of Tweedle Dee's logic, may be seen to cling to ridiculous superstitions. Some kosher dietary rules, while seeming bizarre to modern people, may be explained by safety measures introduced before knowledge of bacteria, but ultra-Orthodox Jews at Passover are required to limit the contact of matzo with water—until the last day—and during Hanukah, the menorah must be placed against the doorpost, not on the windowsill. Muslims also have rules about food, but their most puzzling restrictions involve women's hair, i.e., making sure it is never seen in public. Did Muhammad have a phobia or a fetish? Should Alice come across him on the other side of the looking glass, the White Knight better be on hand to defend her! Neither are Christians innocent of oddity. Their sacrament of consuming the body and blood of Christ is a peculiar kind of barbaric cannibalism. Being symbolic, I suppose it is not as evil in principle as the Walrus and the Carpenter feasting on their poor little oyster friends.

Anyone who flies has grown accustomed to the ridiculous indignities of airport security. Unless compelled, I do not fly, the one exception being my annual sojourn in Maine to escape the heat of the mid-Atlantic. There I was at the airport, pleased to see there was no long line to go through security, doubly pleased that my boarding pass had precheck. I did not need to take off my shoes or jacket, but as I went through x-ray, alarms went off. No, I had not left my firearm in a pocket or my Samurai sword. A serious-looking agent took me aside and "patted me down" as he might have a detainee, which by definition I was. He turned up a tiny Swiss Army knife that I often keep in my pocket for the convenience of its small scissor, especially on a trip. I confess I have surrendered several of them to these airport vigilantes. When I explained this to the earnest young fellow, he suggested to my surprise that I just bring a scissor. Yes, a scissor is allowed! What possible harm could anyone do with a scissor? Well, with a knowledge of anatomy, I suppose he might sever a major artery.

Why Alice, you should have known!

AGING

- *What You Were Never Told* -

It is a splendid autumn day as I head out for the village, October's "bright blue weather" and the first when I need to take out my fedora. Opening the gate, I smile at the antiphony of the wrens calling back and forth, the chip-chip of the cardinals, the chortle of bluebirds, and the cry of hawks—princes of the sky. The old gate falls against the split rail fence with a thud. On the holly tree beyond, berries are ripening to an autumnal orange. They will be red by Christmas. I back the old Bentley out of the garage and hit the remote to close the garage door. Coasting down the drive, I remind myself pointedly that I saw the door go down, thereby eluding any subsequent uncertainty about it. I will meet my friend Anna in the village courtyard, where we will take a sunny table to enjoy coffee and croissant from the French bakery; we are partial to the hazelnut java. She is a fellow writer who contributes to my blog and has been of considerable assistance with others of my publications. She is younger, but even old people are now younger than I am, as I like to say. We also share war stories of doctor visits, screening tests, and the discomforts that accumulate along with the years.

Anna is a regular in the courtyard, priding herself at one time in the degree of inclemency she could tolerate—rain, snow, sleet, or hail. Not so much anymore. She is on a first-name basis with maintenance staff and shop clerks, and her blog posts each week come under the heading "In the Courtyard." She reports on spying the

Bentley when it enters the parking lot and is alerted to the change of season by my choice of hat. She will be excited to see my fedora today, autumn being our favorite time of year.

The bakery has a delicious apple walnut muffin, also fitting the season, so I take that with coffee and head for the courtyard where Anna has already arrived. I find her chatting with the Hispanic woman who oversees the shopping center for the management company. Her name starts with a *C*, but as it does not come to me readily, I greet her with a generic, "Good morning, my friend." Too late I remember: it is Carmen, as in the opera, but before I hit upon it, my brain has to reject Carla, who is a clerk at the bank. Instant recall is the first aspect of memory to succumb, most annoyingly, to the aging process—names, words. The brain lets them up often after many hours and then only when one is no longer trying to remember. All the old people I know will invariably joke about calling at three in the morning when the word comes to them. No one ever does call.

Adding an essay on aging here, along with the one on dying and euthanasia, threatens to set a dark tone, but it is my belief that recent generations have eschewed the subject too scrupulously so that cohorts of the old enter the last phase of life not having learned from their elders who died without sharing. Let that not be said of me! I have expounded at some length in other essays on the sublime reality of our ultimately timeless state. But as we go about our karmic existence, some practical guidance would help, and there are humorous elements to growing old. The late, great comedian George Burns, who lived a hundred years, made hilarious fun of being ancient. I frequently have cause to remember him bending over to tie his shoes and asking, "What else can I do while I'm down here?" I follow the comic strip *Pickles*, the work of Brian Crane, which captures the perennial foibles of old age in the zany couple, Earl and Opal Pickles. Opal is forever dragging Earl to the fabric store and complaining that his socks don't match; Earl goes to great lengths to avoid getting out of his easy chair and offers ridiculous advice to his grandson, Nelson.

The matter of aging is highly individual, and in today's culture, most people are in denial about the reality. What are the parameters? How does one know? There is the graying of hair, though some people are prematurely gray. There are the wrinkles: purse strings about the mouth, marionette lines on the chin, the furrowed brow, and the jowls. Sun worshippers get these before others, since the sun causes a loss of collagen under the skin. One who wants to remain looking young can use popular options—dye the hair, resort to cosmetic surgery—but these measures are temporary. The truth will out that denial is a foolish and perilous posture. A wise doctor once advised me, "Listen to your body." Far too many modern people believe they will stay young by pretending that they are. Here is what they should know.

The bleach in dye turns hair to straw. Plastic surgery can go wrong, causing hideous problems, and its effects do not last anyway. Running, cycling, tennis, and many forms of exercise are good for cardiopulmonary health but over years will wear out joints. Knee surgery is especially problematic and can lead to infection and lengthy rehabilitation. Artificial knees and hips also wear out, resulting in repeat surgeries. With a healthy heart, an athletic person may end up living out his long years in a wheelchair. The concept that one should continue the activities of youth as long as possible seems reasonable, even attractive. As long as I can do it, I will! No one talks about cartilage.

I did not know about cartilage, the tissue that cushions the bony joints. No one ever told me that each person has only so much cartilage, and no one ever measures this wonderful, essential material. I am not athletic, but I love to garden, and for many years, I kept a vegetable garden about five hundred feet square with all the summer favorites—tomatoes, cucumbers, peppers, squash, green beans— and lettuce in the spring and fall. Eventually, after an afternoon in the garden, I would suffer a backache that I would treat with a painkiller and a good night's sleep. It would always go away in a day or so. I was in my seventh decade when back pain became chronic. Then I learned about cartilage; it was wearing out, wearing away. This is one thing we are not told. Children in "physical education" classes do not learn about their physical selves; they learn to dropkick a soccer ball.

The loss of cartilage is the definition of osteoarthritis, and I learned something more about this condition, confirmed by my older brother. We might continue our usual activities without immediate consequences, feeling as young as ever, as long as the ailing joints are well lubricated; the pain and stiffness set in afterward. Now it is necessary to be careful not to overdo, to forestall the later result and preserve whatever cartilage remains.

The Victorian poet and novelist Thomas Hardy, who was the son of a stone mason, had reason to know about physical wear and tear. In his novel *Woodlanders*, he captured the condition in his inimitable way after describing the bodily abuse of the hardworking woodlander:

> On many a morrow after wearying himself by these prodigious muscular efforts, he had risen from his bed fresh as usual; and confident in the recuperative power of his youth, he had repeated the strains anew. But treacherous Time had been only hiding ill results when they could be guarded against, for greater accumulation when they could not. In his declining years the store had been unfolded in the form of rheumatisms, pricks, and spasms. (Hardy 1998, 31)

In old age, we learn to appreciate gravity, the strength of which we never consider until it has body slammed us to the ground. Old people lose balance more easily, and once one has fallen, maintaining that balance appears as a miraculous feat. With a stiff back, the floor draws ever farther away, and objects falling there harass and bedevil us. Why do they always fall down? Why can they not fall up? No, they are drawn by a great force toward the center of the earth—the force of gravity—so that we must bend with much difficulty to retrieve them. I often find myself wondering whether we are pulled toward earth because the grave is our increasingly imminent destination.

The accumulation of physical ailments and discomforts is the cardinal sign of gathering age; what may come as a surprise is the suddenness of it. Once the body's reproductive potential declines and we are no longer needed to propagate the species, nature is through with us. The immune system that has protected us for so long from illness and microbial disease weakens. Eventually it can turn against us, as I read in *Natural Causes*, written by biochemist Barbara Ehrenreich. She writes about her studies of the macrophage, a certain type of immune cell that may come in the end to have the perverse role of promoting rather than destroying deadly tumors. Other bodily depredations come upon us. Loss of muscle can be self-perpetuating: there is less muscle to use in maintaining muscle. Even smooth muscle, internally, is caused to weaken, accounting for more cases of gastroesophageal reflux in the aging population. The sphincter between the stomach and the esophagus is giving up. Drying and atrophy advance: eyes, mouth, hair, and skin. While I have read of "aging spurts" analogous to growth spurts in childhood, I see rather a threshold crossed into the last phase of life upon which we wake into a state of puzzling malaise and disquieting uncertainty. Each new symptom must be evaluated to rule out the worst case, but the most frequent finding is more evidence of the obvious: the problem is old age—and another discomfort one must learn to live with for an indefinite period.

Modern medicine makes the uncertainty of aging more discomfiting than ever. There are many more tests and screenings that one feels obliged to undergo lest he make the unforgivable mistake of dying unnecessarily, and no doctor or technician wants to be the one accused of missing the fatal portent. The sonogram or ultrasound is the most faulty though popular because it does not expose a patient to radiation. Any unexplained little blip on the screen raises suspicion, causing further and more invasive exploration. The body cries wolf, as we keep hearing, "It is *probably nothing*" with the sword of Damocles hanging forevermore above us. A wonderful Jewish grandmother of my acquaintance once said, "A young person *may* die; an old person *must* die."

The aging brain can be the most capricious organ of the body, creating some of the most frustrating if risible problems, first and foremost that instant recall business. In conversation or other forms of communication, with irritating frequency, a common-enough word is on the tip of the tongue, eluding capture the harder we try. A friend or associate approaches and the name escapes except perhaps for a vague sense of the initial letter. Whether for a word or a name, one goes through the alphabet, hoping to jar the memory, and such tricks may work for anything but "Tchaikovsky." The search leads to the odd conclusion that many synonyms begin with the same letter. For example, the word *spirit* yields *specter, shadow, shade,* or *falsehood,* which brings up *fiction, fabrication,* and *fish story.* If one keeps a sense of humor, gaps in short-term memory can be amusing: you put on your sunglasses, forgetting to take off your readers, or you hunt for the glasses that are on top of your head. You write a shopping list and go to the store without it, go to the pharmacy and forget to pick up your medication, distracted by the greeting cards, or go up the stairs to the bedroom to fetch something and forget what it was.

An odd facet of old age that goes unremarked is the changing perception of time. I have always observed and wondered why, paradoxically, old people who have a declining lifespan ahead of them are so slow, unhurried—should they not want to make the most of the time left? Conversely, the young, with their whole lives yet to live, are constantly rushed. I have decided that for young people, it is their reproductive years that they feel pressed to maximize. What awaits an old person is nothing to rush toward. Time begins to hang heavily as we wait for the other shoe to drop. While a person may move or drive more slowly—often for physical reasons—there is an ironic impatience with waiting for anything. Time diminishes and life wanes, bringing further paradox: a distorted perception of duration, an anxiety to get things over with. This accounts for the phenomenon of the "early bird special." The old folks lining up at the restaurant for a cheap early dinner are not there just for the discount—they would eat just as early at home and go to bed soon after.

Many of the social aspects of aging come as no surprise. The hoped-for stage of retirement from one's career or profession, while attractive, has pros and cons that are widely known and discussed. We recognize that removing oneself from the workforce requires major adjustment, and most of us accept that, in any case, we become irrelevant in the natural course of things. The future does not belong to us, since we will not likely occupy it. What may not be clear to the present generation of the old is that change in today's world races ahead faster than ever. The technological revolution continues to have enormous impact, particularly on older people, many of whom haven't the most rudimentary knowledge of computers. Those who know the basics may try to keep up, but the rules change midgame with every software update. If they have retired, they no longer have a young coworker in the next cubicle to help them.

After I broke down and bought an iPhone, having decided that life as we know it would soon be impossible without one, I attended a free class at the Apple store. Another old man there, who apparently haunted the place, badgered the amiable young tutor about obtaining a printed owner's manual. The concept—that there might be a printout covering the entire capacity of what has become a small brain—was astonishing. A young person will play with the thing, figure it out by trial and error, or solicit help from friends, but such a possibility would surpass that old man even if it had occurred to him. Fortunately, the tutor handled him with admirable sangfroid.

Other areas of the consumer culture are changing daily, which I explored at some length in the essay "Choices." In times past, a person might safely expect to return to a department store from year to year to replace a favorite style of underwear or trousers, coat or hat. Those times are gone, replaced by the rule of carpe diem. When you find something you like, *buy it now!* It will be gone tomorrow. Stock up on the underwear if you can ferret it out from the myriad colors, sizes, shapes, and styles. If your name and address have found their way onto a mailing list of old fogeys, your mailbox will be deluged with catalogs targeting that demographic and offering, thankfully, at least some of the discontinued items.

My sister wears blazers in the spring and fall when the temperature is just right, and she always sports a lapel pin—not a brooch, which is larger, just a small, often seasonal pin of which she has accumulated a good collection. The sale of this item of costume jewelry has nearly disappeared from the stores, and now she laments those that got away. There was the one with pearls for peas in a golden pod and another with a mother-of-pearl moon shining above silver pine trees. She mistakenly assumed she would go back next season and have another chance. Pins can come loose and fall off a jacket, and she has lost some favorites that way. These she bemoans the most, since they are now irreplaceable. In spite of this risk, she continues to wear them—with great care—and often receives compliments from strangers, mostly young women who, admiration aside, would never wear such a thing themselves.

Many of us believe we are prepared for getting old, but the inevitable hardships and adversities, regardless of how we try to project ourselves into their reality, remain theoretical, and that is the biggest danger—believing in our preconception. We may think we are resigned to irrelevance; we have had our days in the sun and have memorized Ecclesiastes. Still one cannot imagine how he will feel the first time he is ushered into the back seat of the car with the daughter and son-in-law in front or the first time a waiter refers to him as "young man." Only an old man is called "young man." Old women are called "sweetie," even more egregiously patronizing!

The ingenuous belief that one will be spared any surprises as one ages, having considered the inevitability of aging with sufficient thoughtfulness, seems to be peculiar to people in their sixties and in perfectly good health who mistakenly think themselves already old. They may be tending in that direction, but most appear to retain a degree of physical and mental vigor, enough not to be conscious of deficits. They still display energy and initiative and most notably resilience. They take these qualities for granted, never imagining that they might tire easily, lose interest in things, and withdraw from social interaction, becoming bored and depressed. People who are not yet seventy, together with agents peddling condos in Florida, are the ones to popularize and perpetuate the rosy scenario of the "golden years."

We should observe that as life span declines and life ebbs, the process must involve retreating from things and that there is nothing to be gained in clinging to what we must relinquish. Were it not for our dwindling energy and interest, we would want to live forever, and as far as we know, no one has.

This brings us to the anomalous nature of healthcare today, as an aging population begins to pour into medical facilities. That bulge of the postwar baby boom is expected to overwhelm the system in the coming years. They will find that the doctors who have not already suffered burnout are no longer taking new patients, and they will be assigned to the youngest partner, a recent graduate from a medical school in Bangladesh established in 1986. They will learn that there is no practical difference between a socialized system and a private one except that access to the latter is severely restricted. The wait times are equal for surgery, emergency care, or simply to see the doctor. The office waiting rooms will be filled with gray heads bent over their smartphones, whiling away countless hours. It will be their misfortune to remember the far less vexatious experience of their own parents when there were still enough physicians, any of whom were able to devote sufficient time to providing a diagnosis.

Realizing that those days are gone forever, this generation will rethink the whole matter of medical care. Not surprising for these aging hippies is the growing interest in shamanism. More to the point is Barbara Ehrenreich's position that she is "old enough to die." Those people who recall how their parents sought out—and paid for—every pill, procedure, and surgery that promised to keep them alive, regardless how infirm, know of their own experience the truth that there are worse things than dying. Given the high-tech advances in medicine, a patient can be kept alive until the largest organ of the body—one for which there is no transplant—decomposes. That would be the skin. With the danger of turning into a zombie, one is forced to conclude that a person can live too long and temper his decisions accordingly, taking care not to block the exits, as I like to say. It is possible that an aging population may not overwhelm the system if great numbers take a pass on medical care.

From a statistical standpoint, when a person has avoided the major causes of death, he or she may have no way to die and yet will continue to age, becoming increasingly enfeebled and demented. For this reason, in medical circles, pneumonia has long been called "the old man's friend." We were not told such things. I am telling you now.

The last phase of this life, its inevitabilities withal, has those times of reasonable comfort and peace when relieved of onerous responsibilities and expectations, one may sit back in an easy chair, relaxed, and reminisce about long-ago days, more easily remembered now than anything recent. My Irish grandfather, a great storyteller as befits an Irishman, was on the porch of a beach house known as Crow's Castle in his rocking chair, telling a fish tale to his chums when he slumped over, dead from a heart attack. Those were the days when one was still allowed to simply drop dead.

Anna and I, having our separate errands on that autumn day, leave the courtyard, she to the pharmacy and I to the car. Where did I park it? Briefly I experience that threat of embarrassment, but no need to wander the aisles in search of the Bentley. I press the remote, and it talks to me. My hearing still acute enough to zero in on the sound, I talk back. "Ah, there you are!" Yes, we talk to ourselves when others are no longer listening. Should anyone chance to hear me, I announce that I am "thinking aloud."

DEATH AND EUTHANASIA

- A Third Way -

It was unusually hot for late September outside of London, where my mother was living. The Michaelmas holiday was approaching when the family was alerted that she had fallen and was taken to hospital from the assisted living apartment where she had lived for the year and a half since my father died. Cutting short any holiday festivities, my siblings and I converged on the hospital with all due haste. Mother was eighty-six. We found her in the emergency room in considerable pain, attendants checking her over and doing all they could before a doctor could be summoned. Had she fractured a hip? Was it the congestive heart failure that she had managed for some time? She was conscious and talking, but before long, she appeared to have a seizure. Nurses rushed in and took off her gown. Before she was moved to intensive care, the last horrible sight I had was of my mother naked and writhing on a gurney.

She was stabilized in the ICU, hooked up to monitors and IVs, and intubated, so while still conscious, she could no longer talk. Her internist was enjoying a holiday weekend with his family and could not be consulted. Two days passed as my mother languished in the nightmare torment of intensive care. No fracture could be found, but there was some hope that an embolism had blocked an artery and, given blood thinners, might be passed. Meanwhile, we kept her company, doing whatever we could think of to make her more comfortable.

On the third day, her doctor appeared. By that time, her kidneys were failing, and she had been on the respirator for days, unable to breathe on her own or speak. Considering her age and the organ failure, the doctor spoke to her frankly, offering two options: they could leave her on this machine or remove the tube, in which case she would suffocate—not that bluntly but words to that effect. Mother, nodding assent, chose to stay hooked to the respirator but not because, as the doctor put it, she was "a fighter." No one would choose to suffocate.

It was clear at that point that she was dying from a cardiac event. As it would have been cruel to subject her to further interventions, the doctor ordered morphine to keep her comfortable. Before the day was over, she had passed away. In spite of my grief in the weeks that followed, I wrote a letter to her physician, thanking him for his part in her care, realizing at the same time, tacitly, his all-too-common subterfuge. There were not just two options: continue the struggle to breathe through a tube or suffocate. His patient was not offered a third alternative, which he could not mention because it is illegal. The administration of morphine at the end of life has to masquerade as a "comfort measure," but all involved must know it is a mercy, a "good death"—euthanasia.

The reality is that every living thing dies—ages ordinarily, then sickens, and dies. We go about life enjoying its comforts and pleasures, while here is this grotesque fly in the ointment: the nagging certainty that sooner or later, pleasure will give way to pain, comfort to misery, joy to grief, and that such a horrific state and none other must be our final experience preceding oblivion or whatever afterlife awaits. No creature has been found to enjoy another fate: to continue living indefinitely or even to die serenely without attendant mayhem of some kind. No creature escapes, not we ourselves or our loved ones, cruelly snatched from our midst, unless we have had the good luck to succumb beforehand. Whatever divine being we entrust with our devotion does not reciprocate it sufficiently to spare us this universal experience. We suffer long, tortuous deaths embellished with terror and prolonged with medical ministrations, and finally, we are wrenched unmercifully from all we have held dear in life.

Oddly, we seem by and large not to wonder why this circumstance must be, why our last moment should be our worst, and why death could not rather be the crowning experience. Religious people may believe that it is until it happens to them. A preconception of death is one thing and quite another when it becomes personal. It is one thing to think of meeting your maker in the Great Beyond and another to struggle in the losing battle for your last breath, one thing to say we have had a good life together and another to watch the hospital monitor as your spouse slips from being into nonbeing. There are those who have been resuscitated and report of death's peacefulness, which is reassuring even if attributable only to brain chemistry. Even where death is regarded as a blessing, it is only because the ultimate catastrophic illness has preceded it by too many days, weeks, months, or years of intractable suffering. As in Tolstoy's novella, *The Death of Ivan Ilyich*, the dying person is relieved that the whole business of death, the dying process, is over—not that he wouldn't prefer to be restored to health and resume his normal life.

We cannot project ourselves into the state of dying; we cannot face death until that "angel with his darker draught" draws close. We dread the interference of doctors, believing it to be worse than natural death, though the notion that one can be left in the end to the tender mercies of nature reflects a certain lack of firsthand knowledge. Still the medical profession has acquired such control over this process that in contrast to former times, a person rarely drops dead from a heart condition but rather dies because the clot buster tissue plasminogen activator, or TPA, was not administered soon enough or, at the age of ninety-six, he or she had refused medical intervention. In other words, it was an accident that need not have occurred. Since a theoretical "death gene" has never been found that would cause the body to stop when the clock runs out, perhaps we need not die, and yet we do. Modern medicine does not save us in the end, though it dictates that when we die, there must be a reason.

In 1994, Yale-trained surgeon Sherwin B. Nuland wrote *How We Die: Reflections on Life's Final Chapter*. His purpose was to help the lay person, from his experience in medical practice, understand the biological and clinical reality of the dying process. Most memorable to me was this concerning the cause of death:

> In thirty-five years as a licensed physician, I have never had the temerity to write 'old age' on a death certificate, knowing that the form would be returned to me with a terse note from some official record keeper informing me that I had broken the law. (Nuland 1994, 43)

The fact is that in advanced age, the body does wear out and at some point loses the capacity to sustain life. It has been shown statistically that if one escapes the major causes of death, after the age of ninety, the only way left to die may be the slow fading away of old age, which is lumped into the equivocal terminology "failure to thrive."

Barbara Ehrenreich's *Natural Causes*, cited in the last essay, describes in detail the many trends afloat aimed at prolonging life or, wishfully, avoiding death altogether—fad diets, marathon running, the yoga craze, vitamins and dietary supplements, and so on. Proclaiming she is old enough to die, she will forgo the routine health screenings so as not to spend her waning time on this earth in medical offices. She survived breast cancer some years ago, giving her ample authority for this decision, and her peers in the older generation will identify with it, but she says nothing in regard to the suffering, the living hell that most people fear more than death.

In ancient times, Greeks and Romans recognized and accepted the more humane solution in euthanasia, while today the best alternative that can be offered is to withdraw life support, allowing one to slowly suffocate or starve. The movement toward assisted suicide was championed by the late Dr. Kevorkian in the 1990s, who went to jail for his activism. Opponents make the apt point that more compassionate treatment of the terminally ill is needed, and if such were provided, fewer individuals would desire this final exit. Their slippery slope hypothesis, however, is a non sequitur. No reason exists why assisted suicide could not be as closely regulated as every other aspect of medical care.

We humans see things in black and white, something in the design of the brain perhaps, the symmetry of nature, all reducible to the magic of two: sexual reproduction, cell division, right side, left side, light and dark, night and day, on and off, binary code. Thus when faced with choices, we tend to look through our blinders and see bifurcations, yet there is always a *third alternative*. When it comes to terminal illness, as in my mother's case, this third alternative cannot be mentioned even though it can put the patient's mind at ease and is, ironically, the one commonly implemented. Giving morphine, which suppresses respiration, to a person who is already having severe trouble breathing is more than pain control. The purpose is to spare a dying patient awareness, but why must we be hypocrites about it? We easily grant our beloved pets the mercy.

Tibetan Buddhism, which has a great deal to say about the subject of death, holds that our suffering redeems our sins, or bad karma, and so is beneficial and should not be avoided.[10] Hold the morphine! This idea resembles the Christian concept of sin and retribution, of paying for our misdeeds, but it seems to me a distortion of the actual doctrine of karma as cause and effect. The doctrine indicates that each action, good or bad, goes forth like a ripple in a stream and cannot be called back from its eventual consequences. "The moving finger writes and having writ moves on, nor all your piety nor wit can lure it back to cancel half a line,

---

10. *The Tibetan Book of the Dead* is an ancient scripture translated for Shambhala Publications in 2005 by Gyurme Dorje, and a modern take on it is *The Tibetan Book of Living and Dying* by Sogyal Rinpoche.

nor all your tears wash out a word of it" (Fitzgerald 1952, 66). In other words, if I sin, it is the effect of that act itself that later comes back to haunt me if only through the coarsening of my soul, leaving me in the throes of ignorance. If I develop a brain tumor, it is not a punishment but the effect of physical causes—the mutation of a gene allowing cells to replicate destructively. Does my suffering in this case redeem unrelated past sins?

Even if we see no need to suffer in order to purge bad karma, we still might want to eschew narcotics in order to be conscious at the time of death if we believe it is a pivotal event that we might influence. If the state of death brings us to considerations of rebirth, perhaps we should enter it with our eyes open, so to speak, contradictory though that seems. Unlike people of the West, Asians go to extreme lengths to avoid rebirth by attaining enlightenment. *The Tibetan Book of the Dead* was written in ancient times as a last desperate means of effecting this escape *following* death. The scripture would be read over the dead person's body by a holy lama, the belief being that one's spirit lingers on for a while passing through certain phases or bardos. If that spirit can be persuaded to recognize the terrible phantasms he encounters as the product of his own mind, his "intrinsic awareness," he may elude the horrible fate of reincarnation. The first such phantasm he will see is the "ground luminosity" that surely must equate to the bright light reported in the near-death experience.

Whatever process, if any, awaits us in death, it would be another aspect of the phenomenal realm, and for a Buddhist, the goal is emancipation from that realm, which can take place only while we have this mind and the potential of its consciousness to know itself. The objective in life is seen as enlightenment, and even the Tibetans do not believe that one must die to attain it, though they seem to feel death is the best opportunity.

The problem of suffering is another matter bound up with a major delusion of our benighted state: time. Pain and suffering are bearable so long as they do not endure or so long as we know they will not endure. To be trapped in our suffering, not knowing when or if it will end, is our deepest fear and torment, yet what traps us is the delusion of time.[11] Intuition tells us that time is a fallacy. We say that it passes, but we never sense its motion. Our every experience occurs in the present; we remember a past and postulate a future, but we never once set foot there, validating the observation that time has not moved. The perception of time is a function of consciousness and may be synonymous with it. The more alert one is, the more aware of time and vice versa. If one is absentminded, time is said to fly by unnoticed. If one is unconscious, time has no bearing at all, subjectively speaking. I would conjecture that the dichotomous nature of our everyday discriminations encloses us as between opposing mirrors, so that what we call time occurs as the reflection of these discriminations, seeming to extend, as in the two mirrors, infinitely into the past and future. Perception ricochets between day and night and back to day, hot and cold and back again, creating our impression of a present, past, and future. Were we to rise above the mirrors, the procession of time, like the reflections, would disappear.

Unfortunately, the idea of time and its passage is as tightly woven into the fabric of our thoughts as the discriminative process that gives rise to it and the ego self that engenders the discriminative process. This mental fabric is a virtual felt of impenetrable ignorance and delusion. The fact that we have no words to describe a reality that does not come and go, that does not pass through time, reveals that even our highest mental skill, language, is predicated on the preconception of time.

A Zen story tells of a master called to the bed of a dying man. The master inquires how he may be of assistance, to which the dying man replies, "Where I am going, no one can help me." The master says, "Let me show you the path where there is no coming and going," upon which, on his deathbed, the man is instantly

---

11. Modern-day physics is slowly converging with Buddhist truth, as observed in Julian Barbour's book *The End of Time,* previously cited.

enlightened. That path is the state of timelessness, which requires that our concept of individual selfhood is also illusion. If there was not a self that began in the past and continued on a timeline to some end in the future, the idea of self to which we cling is false. No one has truly been born, so no one dies. The ultimate misfortune is that our only legitimate hope of facing death with any equanimity lies in first realizing this state of timelessness and egolessness, which, as discussed in the essay "On Buddhism," is in truth our essential nature.

We are able to know our true nature by staying alert to reality, irrespective of axiomatic preconceptions, and heeding our intuitions, even those that seem illogical. The earth appears flat, but it is round; objects appear solid, but they consist of molecules, atoms, and subatomic particles. A person who lives seems always to have been, and when he dies, he seems never to have been. We regard such intuitions as erroneous, like thinking ourselves immortal only to find out too soon that the jig is up. These intuitions are glimmerings in the mind of our true state of timelessness. We do live *forever*, except we then disappear as though we *never* lived. It is our words that lie; the mind sees the truth. Once again, between *never* and *forever*, there is a third alternative: timelessness.

It must be acknowledged that even devout Buddhists, dedicated to their daily meditation, will suffer at the time of death. Only the greatest masters will have attained the control to dismiss pain, as one who said, "Buddhas with sun faces, Buddhas with moon faces." Some have demonstrated the capacity to predict the time of their death or perhaps to *will* the event, like the master who told his monks he would die the next day. When the time came, he gathered them and recited a final verse: "I came from brilliancy, I return to brilliancy. What is this?" upon which he passed away on the spot. For most, without benefit of the profound realizations of enlightenment, the loss of homeostasis, activating the survival instinct, will bring terror and whatever physical horrors attend the pathology of our last days and hours.

We hope to be in the care of compassionate people when we die, those who will give sufficient morphine to end suffering. The laws of society should not gag them. Those who minister to the dying have a hard enough task without being forced into hypocrisy, having to mince their words and self-censor so as not to run afoul of the law. The dying are given a choice to be kept alive with the aid of machines indefinitely or be left to die alone. They are not informed that they will be spared the consciousness of further pain and suffering, permitting them to die a peaceful death.

Both my parents were euthanized in like manner. My father had struggled with colon cancer for eighteen months. Caught in the maw of modern medicine, he was subjected to surgery, radiation, and chemotherapy. He died in hospital as fluids built up around his lungs. He was drowning from within. I stayed with Mother, while my older brother spent all night with our father, finally wresting enough morphine from the staff to rescue him from the agonizing experience of slow asphyxiation. By early morning, he was gone.

Despite the ultimate oneness of reality, we live through such bad times as through the good. If we are thoughtful, we reflect that they are two sides of one coin. When we reach the end, should we have the occasion and privilege of experiencing that ground luminosity posited by the Tibetans, may we be able to say, "It is only the nature of my own mind, the universal mind." Then with the Persian, let it rest.

> And when thyself with shining foot shall pass
> Among the guests star scattered on the grass
> And in thy joyous errand reach the spot
> Where I made one—turn down an empty glass!
> (Fitzgerald 1952, 78)

THE PHASES OF LIFE

- *What's It All About?* -

It is impossible to consider the phases of life with any understanding or coherence until one has arrived at the last one. Only then do we have the dubious pleasure of looking back upon them as from afar, and so many people, reflecting on the legions who have come and gone before them, begin to ask what life is all about. As I implied in "The Sexual Theory of Everything," we can extrapolate from the science of our origins that life is recognized as the capacity of self-replication, but that describes it only by definition, while in the question of what it is about, we must infer considerable angst. Sir Arthur Conan Doyle, who died in 1930, offers an example. Drawn to spiritualism in his last years like many in that generation in the wake of World War I, with its incredible devastation and loss of life, he pondered the question in his mystery story, "The Cardboard Box," the convoluted tale of a love triangle ending in double homicide by the cuckolded husband. In the end, his immortal character Sherlock Holmes asks,

> What is the meaning of it, Watson? What object is served by this circle of misery and violence and fear? It must tend to some end, or else our universe is ruled by chance, which is unthinkable. But what end? There is the great standing perennial problem to which human reason is as far from an answer as ever. (Conan Doyle 2003, 396)

That epitomizes the matter for most people for whom life *must* have a meaning. Many find it in theistic religion; others embellish upon family ties with a kind of humanism or plaster an acceptable rationale onto scientific theory. The agnostic is satisfied with not knowing: meaning exists, but since we cannot know it, why bother? In my essay "On Buddhism," I offer the sublime realism of Buddhist thought that the meaning of this experience is more profound than we commonly imagine. Here in this essay, I address the mundane.

A person should not have to wait for old age, when health and well-being deteriorate, to start wondering about life. Those who do are unlikely to have sufficient time to ponder the matter. Still, having reached a proper vintage myself and been graced by good fortune with ample time for contemplation and observation, I hope to convey what I see looking back at it all, not in the personal sense of a recollection but more to the general benefit. In several prior essays, I suggested that the phases of life are predetermined by sexual reproduction. Not unlike all such animals, puberty in the human species ushers in the mating phase and then nesting, and as soon as the nest is empty, nature is done with us. There follows the long period of gradual decline, especially long for humans who seem to think they should, for no earthly reason, live forever.

The earliest phase of life is fascinating and much studied. The human infant is perhaps the most helpless and dependent creature on earth, and it is impossible to overstate the importance of those years to the sort of person an individual will become. A baby cannot understand or talk, cannot express his needs or sensations except by crying, and cannot stand and walk. He seems happy enough and content in a comfortable crib with nothing to do but sleep until hunger arises, the crib is too hot or too cold, or his diaper is wet, and there is nothing to do except to cry for help. He depends for every small need in life upon devoted parents, whom he exhausts with his dependency. Parenting requires the most extreme patience, and I must say that while most parents I have known understand this fact, few seem to reflect on the terrifying and frustrating experience of infancy from the infant's point of view. Conjure if you can the infant's anxiety and frustration, however brief, in a stage of helplessness lasting years. That the experience is not remembered into maturity does not lessen its intensity but may only serve to leave parents, gratefully amnesic for their own experience as infants, less compassionate.

Accompanying that anxiety and frustration are the fear and anger that must be faced and properly managed in childhood, despite being the most problematic. A plethora of advice is on hand for dealing with a child's temper or anxieties, which cannot be habitually suppressed. Like a lid on a boiling pot, the repression of emotions leads to their boiling over and a future of trouble. Too many parents, concerned for their own comfort or convenience, haven't the maturity to implement effective methods, and personality disorder, through ignorance or poor example, is passed along the family tree.

Even with the best intentions, a parent may be seriously misguided. My mother, for example, inherited her Irish father's fierce temper, which she acknowledged and with which she struggled. Determined that none of her three children would be so afflicted, she forbade us to express anger in any way. The injustice of this policy escaped her notice. From our point of view, she allowed herself to turn her fury on us while we were bound to stand mum. For my siblings and myself, the psychological and psychosomatic results were predictable and long-lasting.

Having lived long enough to have observed a few generations, I have to say that perhaps the most treacherous pitfall for families are the fads in parenting, which nowadays seem to change faster than the baby's diaper. When people were more religious, they adhered to the biblical template for raising children, "Spare the rod, and spoil the child." By the twentieth century, methods became far more lenient, and midway through the century, a new bible was widely adopted, *The Common Sense Book of Baby and Child Care,* the 1946 book by pediatrician Benjamin Spock. The good doctor was famously, albeit unjustly, criticized for encouraging "permissiveness" when, in the 1960s, a crop of young hellions turned polite society on its head. A strong influence on many, Spock was misunderstood by many, but the moral is that parents should retain a degree of skepticism when it comes to the advice of experts. Humans are social animals similar to their best friends, the canines, and my view is that children are altogether like puppies. Treating them as such, a parent cannot go far wrong. Like puppies, children are eager to please and belong, so parental disapproval may serve as incentive enough to foster good behavior.

In no time at all it seems, children reach puberty, and a most dangerous phase of life begins. Before their brains have fully developed, their bodies are flooded with mating hormones. Boys are in the most danger, given the effects of testosterone, which many studies link to aggression. During this period, any tendency toward mental illness may show up. Adolescents, in their prolonged dependency, require careful guidance by thoughtful parents, the primal drives to mate being as compelling in humans as in other animals. I have observed that the hardest thing for parents may be to trust in the effects of their influence during their children's formative years. A rebellious teen will shout and curse and storm out of the house, vowing never to return, and his horrified parents will be convinced that all those years of nurturance were for naught. A monster has resulted! If there is a sound, loving relationship, rebellion will pass, and the impact of childhood influences will come out, though it may take a few years of patient forbearance.

I once knew an Asian man who had a lovely wife and two delightful children, a son and a daughter. At age thirteen, the girl became balky and defiant, to her father's chagrin. I asked him how he reacted to his daughter's rejection, and he replied wistfully, "I cry." In his beguiling, inscrutable Asian manner, he was smiling. He knew this phase would pass, and an older daughter would return to delight him. With patient humility, he trusted the foundation of their bond to hold fast in the long term.

My nephew was an intelligent child, and while my brother was a dependable and compassionate father to him, his parents divorced. When my nephew reached adolescence, wary of the deleterious effects divorce may have on children, my standing advice for successfully navigating that phase became, "Foolish is one thing; stupid is something else." He understood, eluded stupid mistakes, chose his mate wisely, and is now an excellent father himself.

Like the majority in every generation, he followed the natural path. As surely as the sun rises in the east and is seen to traverse the sky, the young will pair off in accordance with tribal custom and launch into the nesting phase. With luck, the couples will be sufficiently compatible to establish a stable family and stay united for the many years of child-rearing. This phase, young adulthood, is considered the prime of life, in the course of which what we formerly belittled as ancient aphorisms begin to reveal the wisdom that accounts for their durability: "don't borrow trouble," counseling us not to worry about the uncertain future, "all things in moderation," advising against extremes, "don't put all your eggs in one basket" because "a fool and his money are soon parted," and the Golden Rule—words to live by in hope of safety and serenity.

From my point of view, fifty-five is the prime of life, the perfect age. At this point, a person is still young enough to enjoy the fruits of some years' experience. The bloom may be off, but one has matured like a vintage wine or well-cured cheese, and maturity is the key word if not to ensuring success at least to avoiding all-too-common pitfalls. Good judgment, prudence, self-discipline, and humility are the salient traits of the mature person and a brief description of good character. The good fortune to possess these qualities is not the common lot, and the reason lies in the enormous impact of parental example.

People from the most dysfunctional families, against which they rebelled strenuously, repeat their parents' patterns as adults. Ironically, they will marry and have their first child at the same age as their parents, live in the same community, and continue to struggle with their elders at awkward, acrimonious holiday dinners. Unwittingly, they duplicate their parents' arrested development and, being in denial, remain unaware that they are at liberty to break free. Blessed be the ties that bind? It is the rare individual capable of outgrowing his parents in a significant way. Even uprooting geographically is not foolproof if those family ties are a veritable bungee cord.

Emblematic of the next phase of life is the "empty nest," following the departure of offspring for college or careers, much like baby birds as soon as they are able to fly. I have observed that even gay couples or others without children have a similar experience of this phase. There is boredom and restlessness, an itch to travel, remodel the house, or divorce after decades of marriage. The most consternation, though, after the children leave home, still lies where a parent has been heavily invested psychologically. A good number of the young people I know in this generation have been horribly burdened by an overbearing parent, usually the mother. That may seem a sexist stereotype, but it is rooted in the traditional division of labor that even now requires a woman to devote her best, most creative years to children. By the time they are grown, she may have forgotten what else there may be to life and be too old to redirect whatever energy she has left. Pity her poor children, bound by their mother's apron strings while trying to fulfill their own independent lives as adults.

Grandchildren may benefit from the care of these attentive and engaged older women. There is wisdom in the practice of societies, such as those of Eastern Europe, where children are raised by grandparents so that mothers may return to work. Grandparents are more experienced, and mothers can continue to bring in family income.

An opposite phenomenon is seen today with many parents, who have been eager for the nest to be empty, finding the nestlings regrettably unable to fly, called a "failure to launch." There appears to be a confluence of factors, economic and cultural, inhibiting the maturation of young people and keeping a portion of them from gaining the expected independence. Whether it is failure in school, subsequent unemployment, drug abuse, or another cause, they fall back upon reluctant parents who, instead of retiring to the beach house, continue into old age still supporting their offspring. Where funds are wanting, the return of grown children to the old homestead can be burdensome to everyone, though the multigenerational household is common in some societies, especially when times are hard. Another aspect of this situation is the longevity of elders who must be cared for along with dysfunctional young by those caught between, the so-called "sandwich generation." Stress of this magnitude over the long term is killing, without doubt.

At this point, I must digress to belabor the obvious: one's experience of life's final phase, dealt with in the earlier essay on aging, depends to a large extent on what has gone before and to what degree one has had control of it. People can be born with challenges, physical or mental, that may impair them in some degree. Even a person's social class or cultural heritage may have lasting effects for good or ill. If one has been blessed with any capacity for rational decisions, moderate behavior, prudence with respect to health as well as money, and a cautious eye to the future, there is every chance of his entering old age with a degree of comfort. That may seem a tall order for the generation that thought their government would provide adequate security. In the United States, senior citizens trying to survive on their pittance from Social Security struggle daily, hearing the echo of Ebenezer Scrooge, "Are there no poor houses?" Wiser ones were guided by Murphy's Law and set aside ample savings for their support in old age, ensuring their comfort while averting the fear of becoming a burden on loved ones.

Having entered the last phase of this life, I can write about it firsthand. While many people decry the first signs of aging—the graying hair, arthritis, teeth wearing down, decline in vision and hearing—it was only at age seventy that I was sharply aware of a change. Until then, I could still carry on as usual, retaining the resilience to spring back from overwork or illness. After seventy, that resilience is gone, and I must be careful in what I attempt, mindful of the potential aftereffects. According to my chiropractor, it becomes a delicate matter of balancing just enough exercise to stay limber but not so much as to cause more damage.

In spite of physical deterioration as the years advance, many people, perhaps most, will protest that they remain the same person, unchanged from the beginning. The attitude is rooted in an insistence on the notion of an individual, immortal soul that continues throughout life and even afterward. I beg to differ, especially now that I have reached that point from which I have the perspective of a long hindsight. Looking back objectively with a clarity never before available, I am a stranger to my former self, not merely an older version. I believe that like all perceived reality, we ourselves come forth anew in each instant, changed imperceptibly. The accumulation of these changes becomes noticeable as we pass to each successive phase of life.

As you have read this far in my ruminations, you know that I incline toward trusting my intuitions even when they seem irrational. Now a septuagenarian, intuition is telling me, as I watch my great-nephew, age two, that I was never a toddler. Rationally, I understand that others my age will say that they were once young and strong. My intuitive feeling of selfhood is that I am not young and strong, while the self that once was young and strong was another person.

How do we answer Sherlock's question? What is the solution to that "great standing perennial problem," the meaning of life? A myriad of humankind has come and gone upon earth. "Dust into dust and under dust to lie, sans wine, sans song, sans singer, and sans end" (Fitzgerald 1952, 52), as the Persian has it. What was the point in this rising and falling tide of life, personally or collectively? The answer is highly individual. The devout may find meaning in serving God by helping one's fellow man, though the fanatically devout may believe they serve God through terrorism. To a wealthy person, the meaning of life may be the size of his legacy. A creative person might see it in the products of his art, or he may have been creative in another sense, leaving lots of grandchildren.

I suspect that most people never stop to think of such matters. They live day to day, tossed about by emotions, the neurochemical tides in their brains, like so much human flotsam, and eventually die with that look of horror depicted so well by Michelangelo on the faces of the damned.

To me, the meaning of life is none of the above but to use the gift of human consciousness to search reality to the deepest depths of which one is capable after learning what the wisest minds have taught. Having started out as an evangelical Protestant and ended a Buddhist, I have been eager in my old age to elucidate the tenets of Buddhism for the many lost and struggling souls who might be persuaded. That was the aim of my first book, *Conjuring Archangel*, and the mission of the Great Physician, Buddha himself, who sought to cure the suffering and grief of the human condition through his teaching and the assurance of his enlightenment. He was not just a "woke" person in the modern parlance of the street; he was the man who *awoke*.

In the final analysis, based on my Buddhist beliefs, I would tell Sir Arthur that "human reason" will never provide the meaning of life, never tell us what it is all about. Reason explores only the superficial layer of reality, and regardless of what it reveals, there is a depth it will never penetrate. There lies the paradox of all-encompassing, ultimate reality, "the eye that does not see itself." You already know where it is.

Epilogue

As a young schoolchild, my first exposure to essays came with the writings of Ralph Waldo Emerson in a volume that stood on the bookshelves at home. One in a collection that included the plays of Shakespeare, poems and stories of Edgar Allen Poe, *Ivanhoe, Treasure Island, Robinson Crusoe,* and other works, this volume was titled *Emerson's Essays.* The son of a Unitarian clergyman, Emerson was himself ordained, though he served only briefly as a pastor. Nevertheless, many of his essays read like sermons with titles such as "Prudence," "Heroism," "Manners," and the more famous "Self-Reliance," "Nature," and "Compensation." I was particularly impressed by the latter, which may explain my much later attraction to Buddhism and its doctrine of karma.

Despite the fact that Emerson's most productive years were in the mid-nineteenth century, I do not recall having any difficulty with the language and style of his writing. His themes were universal, often contentious, as he argued against traditional religion. Like his younger friend Thoreau, he was a transcendentalist, asserting his belief that God reveals himself in nature. Such philosophical ideas are if not immortal at least timeless, not of a kind to become dated. Much later, referring back to those essays, I struggled with the antiquated words and quaint arguments. Language evolves, and the further backward we look, the more incomprehensible it becomes to us. Society changes as well, and as we adapt, those bygone days recede and become strange. From the twenty-first century, the English of the nineteenth fades slowly into obsolescence.

In time, even the best works of the most beloved writers become outmoded. William Shakespeare is a prime example. To the untutored modern ear, the original text of a Shakespearean play is cryptic at best. Coming down nearly five hundred years from Elizabethan England, the language of the Bard sounds almost foreign albeit poetic. While the penetrating insights of the plays into human nature and social interaction have procured their eternal relevance, modern theatre companies that perform them have long been at pains to hold their audiences, aware that a growing proportion have trouble understanding the vocabulary and syntax. It has long been common for Shakespeareans to perform in modern dress, a device that is no doubt helpful and may change the context to something more currently familiar. An early example of such a confounding production was staged in 1923 by the Birmingham Repertoire Theatre in England: *Cymbeline*, produced by Barry Johnson. The 1996 film version of *Romeo and Juliet* changes the context of that play markedly, using Shakespeare's words but moving the action to Verona Beach and depicting the Montagues and Capulets as feuding Mafia families. For that matter, Leonard Bernstein's *West Side Story* is the most famous and freewheeling adaptation of the same play.

A writer may aspire to reach out to a long posterity, but realistically, we address our contemporaries. In no form is this more true than the essay. Often resembling the editorials in the daily newspapers, the essay adds to the current conversation, becoming irrelevant soon thereafter. A few essays in this collection were drafted years ago and had to be seriously reworked to make them appropriate for the changing times. Since times continue to change, I am aware that this book may not have a long shelf life, though I must hope that the style itself might continue to appeal.

Even with clairvoyance, we can have no certainty as to the future. Prophecy is a dubious art. It may seem highly unlikely, for example, that today's passion for sport will someday wane, causing schoolchildren to forsake the soccer team for piano lessons, but who can say? Furthermore, there may be dire events that are largely unforeseen or that society is loath to face. These are turning up even now in the results of climate change and, as I write, a pandemic brought on by a coronavirus. The question of population growth, which I bring up in several essays, will become moot if multitudes are drowned by rising seas, burned in raging wildfires, or, as is already the case, killed by a highly infectious pathogen.

Nothing is certain. As the pandemic crisis ramped up and it became obvious that without immunity or vaccine, our only defense lay in the draconian methods of isolation used against the plague for hundreds of years, there came plausible predictions of worldwide economic collapse. Our lives would never be the same after such a catastrophe, and human behavior would change. Human life and human nature, whatever the state of society, have not been subject to evolution since our clever brains set us apart from other animals. A point I harp on in these pages, echoing the ancient Socratic advice to "know thyself," is our failure to acknowledge or appreciate our intractable nature. No, we are not likely to change but to return to our old ways as soon as danger is passed.

The essay that dares to be topical is at risk of being run over by the wheels of time. Should the tenuous, delicate architecture of the internet collapse by virtue of cyberwar or authoritarian misrule, my complaints about the Tower of Babel in the essay "Communication" would expire along with the problem I call "proliferitis" in the essay "Choices." In short, the civilized world would plummet into a barbaric condition: back to three flavors of ice cream, no yogurt, and no phone, smart or otherwise.

Nothing is certain except perhaps the cyclical nature of trends. Facial hair was the style for men before the twentieth century. It fell out of favor for generations, returning as the centuries changed again. Blue jeans, which I decry in the essay "Appearance and Reality," have been obligatory since the sixties, yet while still worn by men on every occasion, I increasingly see women in skirts again.

As my intention has been to capture and convey universal and timeless truths, to get to the root of things, some of the guidance in these pages may have lasting value despite changing times. If I have succeeded in offering this advice in a sufficiently palatable form, some few souls having read it may be helped. At least they will have something to chew on.

That I have strong feelings on these subjects will be clear to readers, whom I hasten to assure of my effort to mollify the intensity. My keenest incentive is that certain things need to be said now more than ever. In my lifetime, as globalization has moved the civilized world higher on de Chardin's upward spiral, even toward its apogee of one world, there is the coincident risk of collapse, signs of which begin to appear. Are those distant rumblings we seem to hear the thundering hooves of prophecy, slowly cracking the global order on which we now depend? In a thoughtless haste to unite humanity, may we not have willfully ignored the impassable chasms that separate groups of people— East from West or male from female?

The modern era has brought about the strangest ironies: speedier communication making it harder to communicate, overwhelming options in every market from groceries to marriage, leading only to indecision, advances in medicine while healthcare regresses to the day when the hospital was the place to die, not to heal. Without the vantage point of age and the tradition of respect for elders, today's young people appear to be unaware of these incongruities. They neither understand the complexity of their lives compared with former generations nor that life need not be so.

I argue for realism, temperance, and caution as in the Hippocratic oath *primum non nocere*. An ancient Taoist saying has it that "the sage keeps to the deed that requires no action." While paradoxical, it is good advice. Think first and wait. Often, no action is required. "Spring comes, and the grass grows by itself." When needed, you will act wisely. Such was the creed of conservatism before moderation was squeezed out by extremists. True conservatism once meant having an inclination to conserve traditions combined with a reluctance to implement radical changes or experiments without careful consideration of possible consequences. It is all but snuffed out in today's world, making me a fossil. Some readers may at least find in these essays the voice of sanity. I will be gratified if they join in my hope that mine is not the last such voice we hear.

Bibliography

Barbour, Julian. *The End of Time*. Oxford: Oxford University Press, 2001.

Capra, Fritjof. *The Tao of Physics*. New York: Harper Collins, 1992.

Carroll, Lewis. *Through the Looking-Glass*. Mineola, NY: Dover Publications, 1999.

Catton, Eleanor. *The Luminaries*. London: Granta Publications, 2013.

Champion, W. Grey. *Conjuring Archangel: Chronicle of a Journey on the Path*. Bloomington, IN: Balboa Press, 2015.

Conan Doyle, Sir Arthur. *The Complete Sherlock Holmes Vol, II*. New York: Barnes & Noble Classics, 2003.

Cyrulnik, Boris. *The Dawn of Meaning*. McGraw Hill, 1992.

Damasio, Antonio. *Descartes, Error*. New York: Penguin Books, 1994.

deChardin, Pierre Teilhard. *The Phenomenon of Man*. Harper & Brothers, 1959.

Dickens, Charles. *A Christmas Carol*. New York: Bantam Classics, 2009.

Dickinson, Emily. *Collected Poems of Emily Dickinson*. Digireads, 2016.

Dillon, Brian. *Essayism: On Form, Feeling, and Nonfiction*. New York: New York Review of Books, 2017.

Dorje, Gyurme (translator). *The Tibetan Book of the Dead*. London: Penguin Books, 2005.

Ehrenreich, Barbara. *Natural Causes: An Epidemic of Wellness*. New York: Twelve, 2018.

Fitzgerald, Edmund. *The Rubaiyat of Omar Khayyam*. Garden City, NY: Garden City Books, 1952.

Glover, David, and Cora Kaplan. *Genders: The New Critical Idiom, 2nd Edition*. London and New York: Routledge, 2009.

Goddard, Dwight, editor. *A Buddhist Bible*. Boston: Beacon Press, 1938.

Greene, Brian. *The Fabric of the Cosmos*. Toronto: Vintage Books, 2003.

Hardy, Thomas. *Woodlanders*. London: Penguin Classics, 1998.

Hubbard, L. Ron. *Scientology: A New Slant on Life*. Bridge Publications, 2007.

Johnson, Allan G. *The Blackwell Dictionary of Sociology*, Second edition. Malden, MA: Blackwell Publishers, 2005.

Jourdain, Robert. *Music, the Brain, and Ecstasy*. New York: William Morrow, 1997.

Kapleau, Philip. *The Three Pillars of Zen*. New York: Anchor Books, 1989.

Lorenz, Konrad. *On Aggression*. Boston: Mariner Books, 1974.

Middleton, Richard. *Studying Popular Music*. Buckingham, England: Open University Press, 1990.

Nuland, Sherwin B. *How We Die: Reflections on Life's Final Chapter*. New York: Knopf, 1994.

O'Cadhain, Martin. *The Dirty Dust*. New Haven: Yale University Press, 2016.

Paine, Thomas. *Common Sense*. New York: Coventry House Publishing, 2016.

Reps, Paul, ed. *Zen Flesh, Zen Bones*. Tuttle Publishing, 1998.

Restak, Richard. *The Brain Has a Mind of Its Own*. New York: Three Rivers Press, 1993.

Rinpoche, Sogyal. *The Tibetan Book of Living and Dying*. San Francisco: Harper Collins, 2012.

Smith, Huston. *The Religions of Man*. New York: Harper Collins, 1958.

Solomon, Maynard. *Beethoven*. New York: Schirmer Books, 1977.

Spock, Benjamin. *The Common Sense Book of Baby and Child Care*. New York: Duell, Sloan & Pearce, 1946.

Stone, Eleanor Spencer. *Franz Liszt: The Artist as Romantic Hero*. New York: Little, Brown, 1974.

Suzuki, Shunriyu. *Zen Mind, Beginner's Mind*. New York: Weatherhill, 1970.

Tannen, Deborah. *That's Not What I Meant: How Conversational Style Can Make or Break a Relationship*. New York: William Morrow Paperbacks, 2011.

Tolstoy, Leo. *The Death of Ivan Ilyich*. London: Penguin Classics, 2008.

Vance, J. D. *Hillbilly Elegy*. New York: Harper Paperbacks, 2018.

Author Bio

The author, known by the pen name W. Grey Champion, has always loved writing, although he did not pursue it as a profession. His career did allow him to cultivate that passion and, in retirement, to indulge it.

Ruminata is Champion's third publication. The first, *Conjuring Archangel* (2015), is a work of creative nonfiction on the subject of Buddhism, and the second, *More Than an Actor* (2018) is a biography of British actor Jeremy Brett. Champion has also written a weekly blog, "From the Moleskine," for many years.

www.ingramcontent.com/pod-product-compliance
Lightning Source LLC
La Vergne TN
LVHW091543060526
838200LV00036B/690